ENDORSEMENTS

"So much depth, yet simple and easy to understand. So much experiential knowledge on prayer. This is certainly one of the books on prayer that would ignite one's passion for prayer and inspire a life of prayer."

– Ama Ofosu-Koranteng, Pastor (Pilgrims Chapel, Pretoria)

"This book comes to grips with the real work of praying not in vague theoretical concepts, but in clear guidelines for personal initiative. The book is simple and straightforward and yet insightful. The master's mandate to always pray and not faint need not be lost to those who will take to heart the counsel found in this volume."

– Reverend Ransford Obeng (Calvary Charismatic Center).

"I have read this book several times, and my prayer life and my understanding of the dynamics of prayer have been enriched for the better."

– Ato Yawson, Author of "Men Are! Wives Become"

"I came across the book as one of the books on prayer, but glancing through it never ended with me reading cover to cover. It became my prayer guide, and the inspiration was worth reading. I then became a witness of testimonies and coincidence as a result of prayer when I moved from standing afar to admire prayer to where I learnt to prayer myself."

– Richmond – UK

"A profound 're-kindling' reading experience. A source of encouragement and moral support. The consequence of it is the fruit of blessings and curses. Spiritually uplifting, a wake-up call to a 'sleeping' or 'slumbering' Christian.

– Dr. Yaw Agyei-Henaku

"I have always looked out for practical and theoretical Christianity. I first thought it was to teach theory until I realized that the experiential knowledge and information in this book makes you want to do it yourself to have godly encounters. I look forward to another book from the author."

– Mary Gyamfi, Educationist – Kumasi, Ghana

I Did it by Prayer is a timely one. This book deals with how to use prayer to attain your God-given ambitions and aspirations in fulfilling one's destiny in life. Many have destroyed their destinies because of their ignorance of spiritual policies, procedures and principles. Laziness, fear and indecision as far as prayer is concerned have denied many the opportunities to achieve their goals. This book is an insightful, inspiring and thought-provoking piece of work. Gabriel is a living testimony of what prayer can do in one's life.

– Rev. Michael K. N. Atisu - Senior Pastor, Living Springs Assemblies of God, University of Ghana, Legon Accra

I DID IT
BY PRAYER

Gabriel Donkor

Publisher

LAING Publishing
www.laingpublishing.com

Second Edition

ISBN-13: 978-1-7338772-0-6 - E-book
ISBN-13: 978-1-7338772-1-3 - Paperback
Printed in the United Kingdom and the
United States of America

*Unless otherwise stated, all scripture quotes are taken from the **New King James Version**; with emphasis added or paraphrased.*

Publishing Consultants

Vike Springs Publishing Ltd.
www.vikesprings.com

For further information or to contact Gabriel please send an email to: gabriel@laingpublishing.com

Gabriel's books are available at special discounts when purchased in bulk for church groups or as donations for educational, inspirational and training purposes.

Limited Liability

This publication is designed to provide accurate and authoritative information in regard to the subject matter covered. It is sold with the understanding that the publisher and author are not engaged in rendering physiological, financial, legal or other licensed services. The publisher and the author make no representations or warranties with respect to the completeness of the contents of this work. If expert assistance or counselling is needed, the services of a specific professional should be sought. Neither the publisher nor the author shall be liable for damages arising here from. The fact that an organization or website is referred to in this work as a citation and/or a potential source of further information does not mean that the author or the publisher endorses the information that the organization or website may provide or recommendations it may make, nor does the cited organization endorse affiliation of any sort to this publication. Also, readers should be aware that due to the ever-changing information from the web, Internet websites and URLs listed in this work may have changed or been removed. All trademarks or names referenced in this book are the property of their respective owners, and the publisher and author are not associated with any product or vendor mentioned.

DEDICATION

To all prayer addicts and those who persistently put themselves to stand in the gap for others and ministries, God bless you.

ACKNOWLEDGEMENTS

To God be the glory for the source of strength and grace He makes available to us. I want to thank those whose inspiration and work has contributed to this edition, especially to my brother Ato Robertson, who inspires me always to put my ideas in print and also helped with typing. Much thanks also to our "Manger" mothers, Maa Tina Agbenuzah and Reverend Ama Koranteng.

To all the fathers of faith whose training and leadership has contributed to my life, such as Archbishop-Elect Salifu Amoako (Alive Chapel Int.), Bishop Alexander Adu Gyamfi (BBT-USA), Reverend Kwabena Berchie (Powerhouse), and Reverend Michael Atisu (Legon Assemblies of God).

Much love also to all the brothers and sisters who are spread across the globe: Mr. and Mrs. Francis Opoku, Reverend and Mrs. Ebenezer Nana Anti, Reverend Patrick Owusu-Agyemang, Maame Joe (Mrs. Josephine Owusu-Agyemang), Mr. Raymond Donkor, Bibiana Donkor, Sabina Donkor and Daddy James and Maa Kate, my prayer tower.

To the family of Alive Chapel and its affiliates, I celebrate you all and say God bless you. To all those who always have desired and asked me for material, I say this is the beginning of another encounter and journey to the things that are open up to us.

My love to my family: Priscilla, James, Jasmyn and Joella for your support and understanding. God is still faithful.

You can always reach me!!!

TABLE OF CONTENTS

Foreword 13

Chapter One: The Key to Prayer 15

Chapter Two: Associated 'P's of Prayer 27

Chapter Three: Pray in the Will of God 35

Chapter Four: Anonymous Prayers 41

Chapter Five: Spiritual Lenses 47

Chapter Six: Praying Always 59

Chapter Seven: Prayer 'AIDS' 69

Chapter Eight: Be Holy 81

Chapter Nine: "Be Still" 87

Chapter Ten: God's Sovereignty 95

Chapter Eleven: You Can Excel 103

Scripture References 108

FOREWORD

Prayer is a force and a lifestyle of the believer and their relationship with their Father (God). To many, prayer is optional since they only use it in times of distress. They only take the trouble to search for God when they need to. They are distant children who hardly hear their Father's will and voice to walk with Him.

Could it be said that prayer is optional? Yes, I have come to realize that prayerlessness is an available and immediate option for the believer who does not pray and, instead, invites other attendees such as misery, failure and defeat, among others, to join them.

Success is never achieved on a silver platter, but it is rewarded to the believer who knows how to get on their knees before God. If you know how to bow before God in prayer, situations can never stand above you; instead, they will bow to you. A person of prayer knows how to take control of the challenging situations they face, including the deadliest (death).

I Did It By Prayer is a call to pray, born out of commitment and diligence to tarry in prayer rather than staying in the knowledge of prayer. Not all who watch or play football are "players." To become a great player, one must commit themselves to work on improving their skills and talents. As one commits themselves to prayer, not only would they become a "PRAYER" but they would be able to stay in communion with their Father in heaven.

This 2nd edition is born out of God's sovereignty as directed over a period of time. The search and knowledge of God are deep and wide, but the insatiable truth that satisfies the soul is real. As you drink deep and commit to learn, know and sustain in persistent and consistent prayer, you are the next testimony about to happen to us.

Connect always to share testimonies as you join me to experience the power of prayer as I did through prayer.

– Gabriel Donkor

CHAPTER ONE

THE KEY TO PRAYER

**"The power of prayer is given to only
the few who actually pray."**

PRAYER is like opening a locked door to a treasure that can only be accessed using the right key. Prayer is both desired and useful. It is a commanded task to all believers who heed the call to find keys for unlocking doors. Prayer is like breath to whoever wants to survive life's tensions, pressures and high traffic in the spirit world.

A Christian (saint) who does not pray is a living dead, disconnected from heaven's power source and can barely produce any energy. The enemy tosses and keeps him busy for nothing.

The key to prayer turns with prayer. Prayer is the fundamental principle of asking and receiving, a communion between man and God.

Ask, and it shall be given to you, seek, and you shall find; knock, and it shall be opened for you. **Mt 7:7 1**

When you desire something from God, you must avail yourself to pray; *then* only can you personally *experience* the benefits of prayer.

For desired answers and results, you must *personally* ask, seek and knock at the right doors, using the correct keys. Many saints hardly *receive* answers as they often and overly depend on others to *ask* on their behalf, which in itself could be deceptive. You cannot enjoy the benefits of prayer unless you commit to praying. Other saints *can* pray with you when you pray.

No one takes medicine for the sick. – *Akan idiom*

ASK: Ask the Holy Spirit to teach you how to pray just as the disciples asked the LORD to teach them how to pray.

SEEK: Task yourself to pray; the more you do, the more you will become a prayer vessel too.

KNOCK: Open doors reveal opportunities and benefits when you find the key to prayer.

Doors of opportunity, blessing, healing and many miracles have keys only accessible to those committed to finding them through prayer. *Finding* is being filled with a desire to pray. Many blessings elude us for lack of access to their locked rooms. This may sound ironic as you wander about for help, as if God habitually disappoints. Truth is: if you desire and seek to find the keys, you commit yourself to the task of praying.

Many resource deposits are yet to be discovered and exploited. We must *dig* deep in prayer to access information to help us take control of our destiny. There are prayer deposits in us waiting to be harnessed and exploited. As we seek, we must also *speak* (declare and confess).

Success, long life, riches and peace were given to you in His salvation package when Jesus Christ died on Calvary's tree. When he ascended into heaven, he led captivity captive and gave gifts to men.[2]

Only a few are aware of this revelation. The few that seek, find it. It is no wonder why Jesus spoke a lot in parables, for those who *seek* knowledge to gain understanding and to take their ignorance captive. "You should always pray and not lose heart." **Lk 18:1 3**

Various hearers received Jesus' teachings uniquely, hence the different effects. The multitudes always expected miracles. The Pharisees intended to trap him by His words, to accuse and have cause to seize Him. But His disciples desired to know their Master's secrets, seeing He often went to a quiet place to pray.

When he finished praying in a certain place, his disciple said, 'Lord, teach us to pray.'[4]

"Your expectation concerning the truth determines what you will obtain. How you desire the things of God proves your dependency on Him."

Jesus taught them how to pray when they desired it and asked. Successful persons have secrets and will only give them to trusted persons who would emulate them. The Messiah used His own example to show His disciples the way so that they could emulate him. They received the key when they *asked* for it.

> *"Pray to become prayerful. The power of prayer is in its practice not in its theology."*

Supernatural happenings resulting from prayer do not occur overnight. Though tiny at first, the desire to pray becomes firmly planted in you by the Holy Spirit. It is sad that most saints *know about* prayer but have not yet experienced its awesome power.

It is one thing hearing great sermons on prayer, even teaching others about prayer. It is another thing practicing to pray. Not all who enjoy nice sermons on prayer are prayerful. Not all who *know about* soccer are proficient players, so it is easy to talk about prayer without actually praying. It is time to stop the talk and get praying.

As we gain more knowledge of the truth of the key to prayer, we must commit to the asking, seeking and knocking principle to unlock doors to our blessing. We cannot be too preoccupied with pressing needs to preclude prayer times in our lives.

Develop a Prayer Pattern [4]

"I believe in prayer, and I love to pray."

And it happened, as he was alone praying, his disciples joined him ... Peter and John went into the temple at the hour of prayer, the ninth hour. [5]

Jesus set in motion a lifestyle of prayer, and His disciples grabbed it. Many instances tell His habitual prayer life (at times with His disciples). He often retreated to a quiet place to pray; in many instances, at night. His ministry and work on earth were founded on prayer. His consistent prayer was the formula for the power and effect of his deeds.

Prayer as a lifestyle needs cultivation, hence the need for a prayer pattern. An astute business person is serious with time being a valuable resource: 'time is money.' Without the discipline to pray, a saint's lifestyle results in a fruitless spiritual (and physical) life.

The disciples developed this great attitude as Jesus made them appreciate the importance of a persistent and consistent prayer life: we see Peter and John's example.

Prayer should be persistent, regular and at *appointed* times, with a disciplined attitude in order to achieve purpose. Whichever period you choose, it is crucial to stick to a set time (though flexible) and a place to pray.

Prayer is an appointment that obliges the other party to honor it: that other party is YOU. Cultivate a disciplined prayer life. The desire to pray should supersede apathy and neglect and create in you the discipline to pray consistently. Most **saints** lack a disciplined prayer life. How can you live for a day or week without fulfilling your appointment with God by prayer?

> *"Though 'hard' to develop a prayer pattern,*
> *a consistent approach grows your delight in prayer."*

It is disheartening when saints regard prayer as an optional activity. In her book *The Hiding Place*, Corrie Ten Boom asked: **"is prayer your spare tire or your steering wheel**?" Most saints resort to prayer only when in terrible difficulties; thus, prayer is just a spare tire. Larry Lea wrote in *The Joy of Prayer* **"every believer may not be called to preach, but every Christian is called to pray. Prayer is our duty**."

Like food and water, prayer is essential for our survival and spiritual growth. We have no excuse not to pray.

The apostles developed a disciplined approach to praying at set times always: an uninterrupted time with God. They prayed at set times instead of teaching, avoiding other activities, so they could be in the temple to pray. Susannah Wesley, the mother of 19 children (including John and Charles Wesley), had her appointment with God every day at noon, and no one dared to interrupt her.

Muslims appreciate prayer appointments better, sticking to their five daily prayers religiously. Why would saints *go for so long* without prayer and still feel *okay*? Though ours is not centered on rituals or religious practices to justify our worship, there is absolutely no excuse for not praying.

Hardly is this *seen* among saints: a Muslim food vendor will excuse herself to *go say* her prayers before continuing service to clients. Until she finishes, forget about being served: an unforgettable lesson for my own prayer life.

"I could not have achieved much, had I not tasked myself to pray. This led to some remarkable personal experiences that could only come by prayer."

No time is too short and no period is special. No matter your schedule, allow time for prayer. You have 24 hours for your appointment with God, and that is *apart* from church meetings. Ask the Holy Spirit to help you cultivate the desire to pray and see it grow into a delightful exercise. The child must have prayer appointments with the Father.

Many saints substitute personal prayer times with church prayer meetings, including *night vigils*, where some just keep wake instead of praying. How do you expect to overcome life's challenges? Prayer sessions are often full of many busy-body spectators. Only a few genuinely and actively pray. Jesus used to pray all night, a period strictly for communing with the Father. Night vigil sessions are opportune times to battle the enemy.[6]

Though hard to develop a prayer pattern, a consistent approach *grows* your delight in prayer. Your daily prayer time produces the harmony of joy and peace to further produce positive changes in your life. Decision, determination and discipline will transform your life into *loving* consistent prayer.

"The agony of choice comes before the promise of change."

During secondary schooling, my preferred appointment was at 3:00 A.M., though tough, it was rewarding. At the tertiary level, another pattern set in—at noon. When I got a job, I had to resort to *go and pray* at midnight.

It took determination and the strength of the Holy Spirit. Indeed, a prayer lifestyle leads to productivity in a saint's life. It has been a long journey, and I thank God: 'I am what He wants me to be.' God should be the judge of your prayer routine, not people around you. Just be sure to *pray*.

A committed praying Christian is very confident. I yearn to meet such who have this lovely praying character. A pastor I admire will not allow anything to interrupt his prayer appointment. You can hardly reach him during his prayer times. He says 'nothing happens by accident,' and prayer is a godly business deserving complete devotion. Some thought he was too spiritual, but it was his priority to enjoy God closely. Though a successful man with a tight schedule, he believes 'the more you stay with God in prayer, the better you can stay with man.' Prayer is true to this effect.

"I learned that greater things could be wrought by daily contact with God than by preaching."
– **David Brainerd, *The Man of Prayer***

Personal Discovery:

I experienced a common canker among modern Christians: we hear much about prayer, yet we are only theoretical. In searching the scriptures, the Spirit implanted the desire for prayer in me. A friend's experience motivated me to explore greater knowledge in prayer, but just when I started enjoying it, many things needed my attention, leaving me with little or no time to pray. Later on, I realized the LORD's call on me to train prayer warriors for victories in spiritual battles.

In secondary school, my prayer desire sadly dimmed, but I was appointed the Prayer Secretary of the Scripture Union. Upon learning how challenging *that* office was at my school, I fervently prayed for wisdom, and I developed a prayer pattern. I was like a man who heard of a gold boom and was heading for his share. I faced spiritual battles and the choice to pray. When I prayed more, I learned greater lessons, and my understanding of prayer increased.

My idea and attitude toward prayer changed from a mere desire into a delight. I enjoyed it and encouraged many to do same. A great zeal and a new fire burned in me. It started as a journey that emboldened me to face many challenges squarely. My revival affected the Scripture Union, and people started on their own to pray and develop prayer patterns, a great landmark in the school's history. Many spiritual matters were settled and many destinies altered. The astonishing testimonies made a difference in mine and many lives.

I could not have achieved much had I not tasked myself to pray. This led to some remarkable personal experiences that could only come by prayer. I found new grounds and levels in life and received keys to *living life to the max*. I had a great awakening. I cannot afford to stop praying.

"Prayer is an investment with greater returns; it is never wasted nor a waste of time."

Many still live on the legacy of other's prayer and what is preached.

"It would be impossible to calculate the failures, the ruined reputation, the defeats, the broken homes and other multiplied tragedies that could have been avoided if believers had prayed. It would be impossible to measure the destruction that could have been averted and the judgment that could have been recalled had God's people seen the need and taken the time to pray. My personal experience through which many lives were saved from the powers of darkness proves the dangers that we face when we are not praying or when we do not pray as we should." – **Larry Lea, *The Joy of Prayer***

Be inspired to find the key to prayer and desire to pray too. I cannot convey all the benefits in this book but to arouse your thirst for prayer. To his disciples, Jesus' prayer patterns were guides and insights into prayer, but until Peter and John tried it, they at least knew the power *in them* to heal. You can only discover this power by *personally* praying.

Modern Christians loath praying and are thus spiritually starved. The *First Aid* of saints is "my prayers" but not "pray for me." Problems seem too big for solutions from God who tasks us to pray. Many want signs and wonders but lack a disciplined attitude towards prayer. Revival only comes when saints task themselves to pray. God *knows* your needs, but pray to affirm your faith in Him.

Prayer has no substitute, so kick laziness out, be purposeful and have a diligent prayer lifestyle: no **fast-foods** section here (one step at a time). Pastors should teach and encourage personal prayers instead of *praying for them*. Elders should pray *with* people rather than being 'prayer contractors.' Prayer is essential and must be given reverence, like other ordinances and not treated with contempt. Very few enjoy the experience of true prayer, but *everyone* is invited. Have a disciplined attitude and be committed to praying.

Be *actors* of your own destinies. With time I have gained a lasting experience. Prayer places you at an advantage to know in spirit what will soon happen—before they occur.

I want you to have the key to prayer. I wish it could be duplicated, like other keys. I am still exploring new grounds in prayer. Endeavor to discover and unlock your treasures and potentials through prayer. Have you caught the *revelation*?

Set your prayer time:

1. Choose a period (dawn, noon, evening, midnight) in your Daily Planner.
2. Allot a specified time, say 20 minutes, one hour, etc.
3. Strictly stick to the period you set. Ask the Holy Spirit for help.
4. Choose a convenient place to pray, not to 'bother' others.
5. Have daily topics and 'be led' to pray on specifics: for Nations, Missions, Pastors, etc.
6. This guide should be flexible and able to adapt to changes.

PRAY UNTIL
YOU BECOME
A PRAYER ADDICT

PRAY UNTIL
SOMETHING HAPPENS
(P.U.S.H.)

CHAPTER TWO

ASSOCIATED 'P'S OF PRAYER

I love everything about prayer, a soul-*satisfying* adventure for every believer to endeavor. Its intricacies and manifold treasures are revealed to only those who travel its road.

Prayer is man's act of communing with God, the medium to dialogue with God. A helpless person contacts divinity to find solutions to prevailing adverse situations and to be uplifted. Prayer should be constant and not at your leisure and convenience.

Prayer establishes our relationship with God, our Father in heaven. We are His children and the sheep of His pasture. When you fail to pray, you indicate you 'are okay without God,' saying: "I am capable of handling my own affairs and helping myself." The prodigal son chose that path and soon regretted it.[1]

Prayer adventure starts with praying. Being the saint's *breath*, no special tuition is needed. There are prayer models in God's WORD and by the Spirit's direction as you *grow*. It is crucial to understand that the ability to pray is inborn, like breathing. "Open your mouth as if you are talking to someone. Imagine talking to God, whatever comes out is prayer." That is my encouragement.[2]

God's church was born by prayer, and one great achievement is her commitment to prayer. Jesus prayed throughout. The early church did the same and fulfilled the great commission's purpose: healed the sick, delivered the oppressed, stood firm in persecutions and grew in the faith of Jesus.

A saint who prays achieves results. A consistently praying church does exploits. A nation that prays develops spiritually and in infrastructure. A nation that stops praying dies from within. The failure of the church results from the low prayer of her individuals, which has adversely affected families, nations and the world. The modern church seems ineffective, resulting in multiple defeat and moral decadence. The prayer power of the early church is missing in today's lukewarm church that easily conforms to worldly standards (the world *hates* God).

If my people who are called by my name will humble themselves, and pray and seek my face, and turn from their wicked ways, then I will hear from heaven, and will forgive their sin and heal their land.[3]

"The greatest thing of all that we are called to do, to change the world, is to pray."
– *S. D. Gordon (What it Takes to Change the World).*

The end is nearer. The church should rise, pray and save many from impending damnation. We should outdo Jesus' example and help shape destinies of men and nations and cause lasting revivals. We need diligent and persistent praying saints to alter evil schemes and bring deliverance to many. We must uphold our birthright and task ourselves to pray (like the early church). We must keep praying to achieve results in affecting our immediate worlds.

We pray for God's provision for our needs, for His strength in our weakness, for His peace to calm our anxieties and for His intervention for our problems. Prayer produces hope and sustains us when we feel like giving up.

Revivals occur when we pray. Positive change is possible if the church prays *down* the Hand of God (power, signs and wonders). We must pray more and less talk. Consistent praying saints affect generations and trust God for positive changes. Like Daniel in Babylon, the most effective way to make a difference is to pray. Jesus' apostles never ceased praying.[4]

This book will stir your spirit to pray and cause massive changes to the destiny of nations. Our generation will shun luke-warmness and establish prayer power to generate a sustained global positive change.

Before starting my training at Kumasi Polytechnic, I prayed for a revival on campus. Though non-resident, I prayed continually for one year until the Holy Spirit's fire caught up with many students. Though He makes all things beautiful, He expects us to 'pray it to pass.' When God's saints pray, depraved situations are reversed.

Praying saints hardly complain but slowly cause great positive changes. The opposite thrives when saints will not pray. Let us pray responsibly and learn more as we grow. God expects us to use His authority in prayer, against the enemy's onslaughts. We are His lieutenants with delegated authority to reign on earth, with a scepter and mighty weapons (prayer).[5]

Prevalent Prayer

PRAY UNTIL YOU BECOME A PRAYER ADDICT

We must persist in prayer. The value of prayer is in praying fervently without ceasing, thus achieving more than seldom praying (albeit for long hours). Persistent prayer achieves objective blessings.

And from the days of John the Baptist until now the kingdom of heaven suffers violence, and the violent take it by force.

Force refers to persistent prayer without giving up on our spiritual pursuit. Jesus' teaching on prayer shows how persistence works: 'though he will not rise up and give to him because he is his friend, yet because of his persistence he will rise and give him as many as he needs.'[6]

Persistence is the attitude for getting answers. We are yet to reach the level of agony of Jesus on Mount Olives, just before his arrest: *great drops* of sweat falling from his body. Sometimes we should go beyond ourselves and agonize in prayer till unchanging situations change. We read of many men of old who did that.

Most Christians are not tenacious in prayer and so lack persistence in all areas of their lives, giving up easily and achieving nothing. Others adopt an attitude of gentility (pretense) in prayer, which denies them many blessings. In *persevering prayer*, you deal with an issue to its conclusion: either causing something to happen or averting an evil. Persistent prayers change destinies, heal the sick and open doors of opportunities.

Growing up where I did, we believed Satan was dumb and only heard when we prayed hardest. It taught me to be persistent and tenacious until I received a specific direction or word. While praying with a group on a mountain top on my 17th birthday, there was sudden rain, but our dire need *kept* us standing in the rain, persisting and agonizing until we *saw* God's deliverance. The violent (in prayer) can take *things* by force.

Your bad situation must change: it will happen when you persevere in prayer *to move* God. Jabez's prayer caused God to change his destiny for the better. Jacob received a blessing after he 'wrestled with an angel' from night till daybreak. "Let me go, for the day breaks." *Not until you bless me.* For his persistence, his name was changed from Jacob (deceitful) to Israel (overcomer). Pray until you get a response.[7]

Your miserable life must change to victory, health, prosperity, success, abundance, etc. Wrestle and attain through agonizing prayer. Choose the best option: become prayerful.

> **"The fact is this: Unless prayer is a vital
> and thriving part of your life, you will never achieve
> spiritual victory."** – *Priscilla Shirer*

We once prayed for a traveling opportunity for a friend. Things looked dim at first, but we persevered, and our persistence made a way eventually. I am hardly satisfied until I see actual results. It cannot be done in pain for nothing. Elijah, a man like us, prayed earnestly that it would not rain, and so it remained for three and a half years. He prayed again, and the rains came.

My point is: **PRAY UNTIL SOMETHING HAPPENS (PUSH)**.[8]

Agonizing and persistent prayer births miracles. Consider praying earnestly, and be resolute. The parable of the woman and the judge demonstrates persistent prayers. The judge finally succumbs to the continuous and irritating pleading of the widow, thus avenging justice on her behalf.

We must petition the great Judge for justice to prevail. We must be importunate and persevering to achieve desirable changes in our negative situations. "Oh God, let me climb up near to you and love, long and plead, and wrestle, and reach, and stretch after you for deliverance from this body of death and failure." – *David Brainerd* [9]

Potency

ONE WEEK WITHOUT PRAYER MAKES ONE WEAK.

'Much prayer produces much power' is a certain motto (in the form of ideas, plans, wealth, opportunity, joy, success, fulfilled dreams, etc.).

Prayer births power to produce results. Praying saints have power over death, odd situations, disease and strongholds. The enemy trembles and tries hard to stop praying saints from firing 'spiritual bullets and bombs' at Satan's cohorts. Praying saints also *have* challenges, but resilience in prayer surely overcomes all opposition and offenses of the enemy.[10]

The enemy relentlessly weighs down a praying saint with many occupations and even idleness just to weaken him, because he is a poisonous entity to the enemy's camp.

We once went in to *evangelize* a certain village but faced resistance to the point of risking our lives. When men entered the bushes and began praying earnestly, the leader of the hostile group had his roof ripped off that evening. Great fear gripped his comrades as one of them died strangely, and these strange happenings provided us with the *opportunity* to share the gospel. The commotion became the perfect setting for us.

Satan has little room to operate when Christians pray: awesome power is released, and the effect is tremendous. It is amazing to see people tremble because of your prayers. We were branded troublesome at school not for any vice but for our prayers *hitting* some people, who even made verbal confessions after we had been to pray. Some literally avoided me for dealing with them in prayer. This effect increases our confidence to pray more.

The church persisted in prayer for Peter's release. Elijah caused King Ahab to fear God. The king of England once exclaimed: *"I fear no other thing except the prayers of John Knox."* Talk of Charles Finney too. The prayers of Benson Idahosa and the potency of his remarkable words in Benin City, Nigeria, clearly depict the powers of a praying man. David Brainerd explained how prayer paved the way for him to witness Christ to American Indians who were not ready to hear about *his* Christ. The effective power of prayer affects generations."

"Prayer is how we see heaven invade earth. It is what opens the floodgates for God to come down and be involved in our everyday circumstances." – *Priscilla Shirer*

Many Christians have fervently prayed to raise ailing economies, create prosperity, cause possibilities and save lives. Bad situations worsen when we fail to pray. The power of prayer can turn growling into glory, poverty into riches, failure into success and cause God's purposes to be fulfilled.

If a Christian ministry is established by prayer, it must be sustained by prayer for guaranteed success. A praying church is a mighty army that saves many lives when they evangelize. "The backbone of my ministry is the prayer warriors." – *Billy Graham*

Summary:

- Prayer develops a relationship between God and us, Father and children.
- Prevailing and persistent prayer brings potent miracles and results.
- The power of a praying man produces confidence and remarkable success.
- The potency of a praying man achieves very great results.

CHAPTER THREE

PRAY *IN* THE WILL OF GOD

"The will of God is the way of life for His living saints."

The will of God is His counsel and purpose that stimulates us to please Him and causes prosperity in everything we do. His will keeps us on track till we cross the finish line.

Three kinds of **WILL** control our actions and activities: God's will (His purpose), your own will (desires and wants) and Satan's will (wishes). Your will is greatly influenced by either God's will or Satan's will: your will is never independent of these two.

God does not force His will; you *choose* to adopt His will. Satan fights God's will for you and usurps your will, just to destroy you, so decide which will rule you. You can achieve God's purpose for your life when you pray and find His will for your life in order to fulfill it. His will empowers you to do right.[1]

If it displeases you to serve the LORD, choose who you will serve, whether the gods your fathers served or the gods of your abode; but as for me and my family, we will serve the LORD. Can you also speak like this? [2]

Identify God's will

God reveals His will in many ways; hence we have no excuse for failure. His prophets revealed His will to the Israelites. His will is *clear* in the Bible, His Holy WORD (the sword of the Spirit). When you pray according to God's WORD, you access His manifold blessings.

Praying the will of God is aligning with His WORD as your measure, which contains His promises and blessings. It is God's will that we should pray; therefore, failing to pray is outright disobedience. God's WORD is key in our lives and prayers too.

"No WORD, no prayer." You may think to be praying, but if it is not based on God's WORD, it is 'not prayer.' And if you hardly pray, you most likely have no faith in God. Prayer is effective when you know the right WORD to apply. Knowing the WORD births the faith to receive answers.[3]

George Mueller fed 5,000 orphans three meals a day: a great example of applying God's WORD in living daily. Mueller is believed to have thoroughly searched the scriptures for the appropriate WORD for his needs, the reason he excelled in feeding the orphans and never lacked. He placed his fingers on the verse in the Bible where he based his prayers. "Then the LORD said to me, 'you have seen well, for I am ready to perform my word.'"[4]

Doctors once declared a friend's state of illness hopeless. While awaiting surgery, he based his fervent prayers on '*I am healed by his stripes*' and '*I will not die, I will live and declare what the LORD has done.*' Not long after, he discharged himself from the hospital and is a living testimony of God's WORD.[5]

Satan's intelligence proves our ignorance. When Satan tempted Jesus with the WORD, Jesus overcame Satan with '**it is written.**' When you know God's WORD, you can enforce it in your life and live in His will to overcome Satan's schemes. Many live in defeat and have countless problems for being ignorant of God's WORD regarding their situation.

'*I am more than a conqueror,*' '*He became poor that I might be rich,*' '*No weapon formed against me shall succeed.*' Explore more of His WORD for your empowerment.[6]

With these, I refuse to experience any ills, and I pray God's WORD in my life daily. For years I used to be ill often, but I *know* "he took away my diseases when He hung on that tree." For anything about my life, I approach God *with* His WORD, and He is *obliged*. God exalts His WORD above Himself and stands behind His WORD to perform it. God *is* His WORD; so when you seek Him with purpose and by faith, His *is obliged* to respond positively and on time.[7]

"God is not a genie in a bottle who answers all our requests, no matter how we are living. The prayers of a righteous person are the ones that are powerful and effective."
— *Priscilla Shirer*

God's will in His WORD delivers from fret and failure, eliminates stagnation and gives insight into His ways, for us to know and fulfill His purpose for our lives. When we accept His will, we *realize* that certain situations are but for a reason and a season.[8]

God's WORD indicates times and seasons for His dealings. As we study it, we know His will more and make it ours. We learn to *walk in His will* and *prosper* in all we *do*. We must pray, live and walk in His will. If we pray in His will, yet we *thief*, *gossip* and *lie*, we nullify our prayers. Learn to reject anything outside God's WORD, which fights your will (His will). Know God's will in order to enjoy His blessing.

Live in God's will

'Oh my father, if it is possible, let this cup pass from me; nevertheless, not as I will but as you will.'

Jesus submitted His will to God. At times our will may conflict with God's will, but the more we pray and study His WORD, the greater we receive the power to live in His will.

We *force* our will on God's will and *suffer* the consequences. We struggle in life when we substitute God's will with our hearts' desires, which *may not* be His will for us. '*He gave them what they asked, but sent a wasting disease among them*' (RSV).[9]

You ask and do not receive, because you ask amiss, that you may spend it on your pleasures. If our request is *against* God's will, He will not grant it.[10]

Endeavor to know God's will about your exact situation and pray in that course. Elijah's prayer (prophecy) '*that there shall be no rains*' aligned with God's will concerning Israel *then*. He declared it, and it so happened.[11]

NOTE: God's will for your life *is* or may be different from others', so do not fret, worry and compare yours with others. Believe that *He makes all things beautiful in His time.* God loves you and has great plans for you if you love Him too. When you know how to pray in God's will (by His WORD), you save yourself frustration, stress and wasted time[12]

I once prayed for an opening and a certain direction, but I later learned that my request was not God's will for me *then*. I prayed earnestly and got no answer until the right time came, according to God's will.

We have prayed for many things and received nothing, but we shall when the time is right, per God's master plan. Learn to determine the right time as well. God our Father *never* denies us any good thing, but our ignorance of the time determines a lot. His delays are not denials.

In God's will is *long life* and *prosperity*; this increases our confidence when we pray to God. When you know and pray the WORD, He is faithful to answer you. Pray God's WORD and will into your family, business, health, education, church and all your concerns. Leaders must study God's WORD and pray thus. When pouring your heart to Him in prayer, **use** His WORD. His WORD makes you pray aright[13]

Summary:
- God's will is our blueprint for *living* to the maximum.
- You will know God's will more if you read and practice the WORD.
- Do not fret about others' progress. Your time and season cometh.
- Prayer is a demand and a command from God our Father.
- Praying persons hardly yield to temptations and to sin.

CHAPTER FOUR

ANONYMOUS PRAYERS

**"The impact of 'unknown' prayers far exceeds
the yield of one kernel of corn."**

Praying for people without their awareness is good. If they learn about it, some people may get alarmed and uneasy while some may get offended. It is expedient not to let them know you are praying for them. Pray anonymously.

When you pray, go into your room, and when you have shut your door, pray to your Father who is in the secret place; and your Father who sees in secret will reward you openly. [1]

The impact of secret prayers is like sowing a kernel of corn. Given proper care, the kernel, buried in the dark earth, produces two and three stalks, which bear two ears. When you examine a cob at harvest, the number of grains on the ears far exceeds the one grain sowed.

The chain effect of prayer far exceeds the yield of one kernel of corn buried in the ground. When you invest time and energy into anonymous prayers, you receive a fruitful return of answers.

"Prayer is an investment of time which rewards the diligent praying person."

Anonymous prayers saved a *backslidden* friend. The heaviness of his heart was revealed to another friend close to him and me. We decided to pray for him without his knowledge, and it worked. He has been on fire since, doing great exploits for God: Satan *lost* him. What a joy! We prayed secretly, and soon he became revived to revive others.

Kobby was a hardened youth who reveled in worldliness and refused to submit to God. In his ignorance, he often joked: 'there will be happiness in hell with lots of famous musicians entertaining always.' None ever thought he could be saved, but unknown to them, a neighbor prayed day and night for his salvation. Kobby got saved, but more than that, *his* testimony also got many others saved; those who thought such a hard knot could never become God's saint. I have *seen* many people I prayed for becoming saved and saving many others. My joy is endless when I see them serving God. Though they least knew my labor, God knew. Some of them converted just when I felt like giving up. For some, it took days and others years. For those still unsaved, it is only a matter of time.

"Whereas the world's resources may not meet everyone's needs, prayer can."

Through such intercessory prayers, the stony hearts of many have been softened and eventually submitted to God. Anonymous prayers with astounding results have saved many from calamities and Satan's bondage. Some pitiful lives became conditions of peace and joy because someone somewhere, without their knowing, cared to pray for them. You may be a beneficiary. Would you care too? You may save a soul.

Intercessory prayers are prayers offered *on behalf* of others. God's Saints are required to intercede for nations, leaders, the unsaved and dire situations for God's urgent attention. Abraham interceded for Sodom and Gomorrah, and Lot's family were saved eventually. On occasions, Moses interceded for the Israelites whose sins so provoked God to want to destroy them, but Moses pleaded for mercy as Daniel interceded for Israel in captivity.[2]

When interceding, you put yourself in the stead of the subject and your labor for a breakthrough for the subject. Peter was thrown in prison to be executed the next day, but the church interceded earnestly for him till an angel was sent to release him. Would it surprise you that someone (you know not) prayed for your salvation and other blessings? Many are *still preserved* because faithful brethren intercede for them.[3]

You escaped that accident unhurt because someone prayed for you at that *hour*. Someone is always interceding for others. I was once *led* to pray for travelers and *against* road accidents on a specific stretch. At that moment, a traveling saint got involved in an accident when a heavy-duty truck hit their vehicle, but he was miraculously saved unscathed.

I understood *that* prayer's *purpose* when he later testified. Certain businesses that are still running can be traced to some people interceding for the owners anonymously.

> *"You escaped that accident unhurt because someone prayed for you at that hour."*

A prisoner for Christ's sake in an Eastern country once said: "we are able to endure the persecution because we know of the prayers of our brethren all over the world." Someone's survival depends on your prayers. When you face challenges and conflict, learn to pray rather than complain: pray about it and see the change as you also take appropriate actions.

Anonymous prayers are more far-reaching than whatever anyone could do. God's WORD is most potent and supersedes anything. Never underestimate the power of prayer. Anonymous prayers took me abroad and gave me breakthroughs far and near. I *dare* you as a Christian to be sensitive to the Holy Spirit who intercedes for us and leads us to intercede for others. The Spirit occasionally *leads* me to pray for people's specific needs hence my desire to be more sensitive to His promptings. Hearken unto Him and experience same.

♪ *Somebody somewhere is praying just for you* ♫ *they may not even know your name, but they are praying just for you* ♪

Just as I pray for people I least know, there are indeed certain prayer warriors I know not, who pray fervently to enable me to do God's work effectively. I recall the experience of two saints, *Josephine Amanfo Sarpong* and *Emeliet Nimoh Dapaah,* sisters I cherish, who through anonymous prayers achieved results in others' lives. Their prayers got someone a job, another achieved financial well-being, plus many other testimonies. Selfless, they are happy when others prosper. No wonder their successful lives are shining examples of God's favor. The Spirit impressed it on my heart that they were praying for me. That encouraged me to do likewise. God *rules* in our affairs, but He expects us to pray, as a step of faith.

We pray for many pastors far and near, and it is amazing to see the effects of our prayers on those ministries. We once prayed for a sister *for* a fulfilled marriage, and God honored our request. We prayed for divine intervention for a couple who had no issue for five years and soon they had a baby. Anonymous prayers achieve a lot.

The story is told of a pastor who dreamed he was in heaven to receive his crowns. After his turn, an elderly church member received more crowns than he, which astonished him. Then God opened his eyes to see the work of the woman which no one ever noticed. She was the praying power behind the success of his ministry. While he slept, she would be awake, praying for increased anointing, new converts and miracle-working power. She ministered to the pastor anonymously and received a double of his rewards. Your heavenly Father *sees* your labor in prayer. He *rewards* openly.

Like the hidden parts of your body, no one may know you, but you do greater works than them whose works are evident. There are hidden warriors in prayer closets laboring for the success of many gospel ministries. If you are called in any way, though you may not be known, continue steadfastly in prayer because God knows. You too can do this and see the effects in people's lives; it is so much joy to see your prayers answered in other's lives.

Summary

- Anonymous prayer selflessly delights in other people's joy.
- Intercession is biblical and achieves immeasurable results.
- God immensely rewards secret intercessors and increases their desire to pray.
- We partner with the Holy Spirit who Himself intercedes anonymously for us.

⟶ CHAPTER FIVE ⟵

SPIRITUAL LENSES

**"What is seen in prayer is tangible;
everything has a spiritual impetus."**

Nothing happens out of a void. The spiritually *inclined* know that physical happenings first occur in the spirit. A man of the spirit judges all things, but a carnal man cannot understand them.

It is written: **Eye has not seen, nor ear heard, nor have entered into the heart of man; the things which God has prepared for those who love him.**[1]

Everything created was contained in God's WORD: He created all things with words. The Christian life is more spiritual than physical, revolving around the Supreme Being, who Himself is Spirit, and Jesus is the image of the invisible God, the firstborn over all creation.

For by him all things were created ... in heaven and ... on earth, visible and invisible, ... all things were created through him and for him ... in him all things hold together ... in whom are hidden all the treasures of wisdom and knowledge.[2]

Everything has a spiritual side, and prayer is the *spiritual lens* for seeing what is yet to occur. The prayer telescope has spiritual lenses that enable us to see far ahead of the riches of God abounding to us. Prayer draws us closer to the revelation of God's affairs and takes us closer to our dreams so that we will not fret but receive what is already ours.

Paul exhorts us to *desire* that **"the eyes of our understanding *will be* enlightened; that *we* may know what is the hope of His calling, what are the riches of the glory of His inheritance *in the saints*, and what is the exceeding greatness of His power toward us who believe, according to the working of His mighty power."** [3]

What is *seen* in prayer is real. "At the point of prayer, the thing we believe God for is as real as it is when manifested physically. A dreamer can almost touch what he sees in prayer. It is tangible." – *Eastwood Anaba, The Tangibility of Dreams*

Prayer gets you closer to your dreams and visions. Your spirit perceives what is yours in the spirit, and by your faith and actions, they get translated into reality. The *future comes closer* when you pray, sensitizing and creating the awareness of how to reach them. Whatever you receive, perceive and cover in prayer, you can possess.

In desperation, you *think* all is lost. Hagar was with Ishmael, her son, in the wilderness when her water runs out. In desperation, she left the child to die, but the cry of the child reached God who opened her eyes to see a well of water nearby. No matter how bad your situation, let heaven hear your cry. PRAY! [4]

We are sometimes so close to our miracles, but we cannot discern *what* to do and *how* to wait. Many **saints** live very pathetic lives. Inability to perceive spiritual things robs you of your treasures and inheritance. While you live *anyhow* without prayer, you block the inflow of your own blessings, etc., yet you search for prophets, in search of those things.

Years back, I lived a life of defeat, illness and other related problems. As I kept praying, I realized in my spirit all that God had in store for me, where He intended me to be and what He wanted me to do. I perceived my legacy and *saw* I had been *robbed* of many blessings. I heard the Spirit say: "if you do not receive them, blame it on your ignorance and not praying." Years passed, and I have many awesome personal testimonies. Some confirm God's WORD as if I knew beforehand.

As I pray more, I *see ahead*. With time, *whatever* I see will happen. By prayer, I discern my origins and my future too. When God has to move me from one place to another, my spirit is aware beforehand, and in the fullness of time, it happens just as I perceived.

For effective *recovery* of your possessions, *know* what belongs to you and *reach* out for them. "You cannot have what you do not know is yours. Ignorance steals but information brings light and possession."

You must contact knowledge in God's WORD for your healing, blessing, prosperity and other successes in all areas of your life as you pray. The King's table is set for princes and heirs. We are heirs and joint heirs with Christ, so we should *live* like royals and not as servants or infants. [5]

Mephibosheth

He was an heir to the estate of his grandfather King Saul, yet he was belittled by *his own* servant for being lame, and his handicap (ignorance) cost him his rightful position.

Not praying can be a handicap that costs you your inheritance. *"Being knowledge handicapped can be a great tool to your detractors."* Satan plays on your ignorance to keep you ignorant. A servant of the royal, Zeba, had seized his inheritance and was rather ruling Mephibosheth.

**"And he answered, 'my lord, oh king,
my servant deceived me ..., because your servant is lame.'"** [6]

Do not allow (a seeming) weakness to master you; master it instead. *Employ prayer.*

Many saints are victims of circumstances, slaves to disease and poverty though they own riches and legacies; yet they wander about aimlessly. They lack spiritual lenses to see and have thus become victims of many ills and vices. Some Christians are pitiable and reduced to beggars for failing to pay the price of discipline in seeking God's direction for elevation.

"My people are destroyed for lack of knowledge."

When David recalled his covenant with Jonathan and he learned of *Mephibosheth*, he restored the 'belittled lame man' to royalty: *"do not fear, I will show you kindness for Jonathan your father's sake, and will restore to you **all the land** of Saul your grandfather; and you shall eat bread at my table continually."*[7]

> *"Your continuous ignorance gives strength to your enemies."*

Jesus died for a reason! Nothing should prevent us from obtaining what God has for us. You might have *otherwise* tried and failed severally, but belittle yourself no more. Move by prayer and grab your legacies in God. You **are** worthy. The woman with the issue of blood had tried physicians for 12 years to no avail till her contact with Truth (Jesus) changed her state. We are not ignorant of Satan's devises so he cannot deceive us. Be in the spirit, pray more, discover the truth in God's WORD for your life and share your testimonies with me too.

Prayer Gives Direction

Many people only circle around *their needs* and achieve nothing. Others make decisions that end in dire conditions. They lack spiritual focus and direction to move ahead, but there is always a way out of every bad situation.

I love how David 'inquired of the LORD' about major (and minor) decisions, hence his many victories; not because he was 'mightier,' but because he *knew* when to move, strike and retreat.

"Therefore David inquired of the LORD, saying, 'shall I go and attack these Philistines?' and the LORD answered 'go and attack the Philistines, and save Keilah.'" [8]

We often let our desires and emotions override God's will and end in deeper troubles. But when we pray, we receive strategic direction for insight to fulfill His will and possess our heritage. We fail for lack of direction to the next steps. Some are capable of handling their affairs and hardly inquire of the Lord. Well, they may succeed, but how much will they succeed? There are two outcomes: either you just succeed, or you have *great* successes.

Lack of direction can be costly, like a blind person with no help. If we do not seek spiritual direction in prayer, we waste precious time, energy and resources; we fail and blame it on misfortune. Some seek direction from any source such as witchcraft mediums and go on to suffer later. We are encouraged to *come boldly to the throne of grace, that we may obtain mercy and find grace to help in time of need.*[9]

You can build your trust and confidence in God and *receive* His perfect direction. I needed favor for admission to a tertiary school because of the '*whom you know*' syndrome. I qualified but knew no one. As I prayed one dawn, God directed me to a woman who helped me greatly. We need His direction, which we receive when we pray.

"*Sorry. I cannot help you.*" People who are capable of helping can so disappoint. We may believe some persons can solve our problems, but it is God who orders the steps of the *righteous*, especially when we *ask* Him. David wrote: "O LORD, you are my shepherd, I shall not want ... your rod and staff comfort me." To wit, 'my God will never disappoint me so I need not fret.'[10]

After my training in Kumasi, I was posted in Accra for National Service, and lodging was a challenge. People *who* could help disappointed me. I reached Accra to register, but I had no place and no alternative but prayer, and God directed me to my mother's friend who greatly helped. She later sent me to *where* I was well received and housed briefly, but when the time to leave was due, I was homeless again. In my spirit I was convinced I would find lodging, so I prayed earnestly, and my able God *ended* my inconvenience.

I cannot explain how these things happen, but I know God's hand manifested them. As He burdens us with His will and direction through dreams and visions, we must walk in it, have our peace in it and live in prosperity.

When he prayed, Paul's intended missions were re-directed. *And a vision appeared to Paul ... a man of Macedonia stood and pleaded with him saying 'come over to help us' ... and ... immediately we sought to go to Macedonia, concluding that the LORD had called us to preach the gospel to them."*

For whatever direction you need, put on the spiritual lens of prayer, and you will surely get it. Seek God, let your prayers and desires fit into His will and enjoy His direction in the midst of troubled waters and dark valleys.

Prayer warns of danger

> **"For though we walk in the flesh,
> we do not war according to the flesh."**

The world is full of consciences *seared with hot iron*. Satan's cohorts conspire against God's anointed, to break our cords and scatter us, always setting traps for our fall. Satan devises *tools* for our defeat, backslide, downfall and disgrace, just as he desired for Peter, but Peter was saved by Jesus. We wrestle with evil invisible beings who desire our destruction. Peter at least knew what happened in the spirit realm: *the thief comes to steal, kill and destroy.*[12]

> *"They will keep scheming, and those who do not pray fall prey to their snares."*

Prayer sharpens our focus and gives us insight into Satan's schemes. Knowledge produced in prayer safeguards us against his manipulations and devices. There was once a praying man in Israel who could reveal all the schemes and plans of the Syrian king to the king of Israel. [13]

Someone once declared evil on my life, at a certain place near my home. The danger zone dawned on me, and I got a direction when the plan was revealed. What happened later did not surprise me. I *knew it already*, thanks to the gift of discernment. Prayer certainly gives us an advantage over our enemies.

> *"When his secret is revealed, he has no option than to bow."*

You may think everything is okay, with no evil implications, but many things are designed by hateful beings to frustrate your financial, material, professional, spiritual and physical progress. You *least discern* even when choosing friends. Unwise and weak sisters often become victims to cruel men who take advantage of their ignorance and leave them worse off. One gained advantage in prayer is to be in '**Known**' about people around me and my environs.

Nehemiah discerned that a certain prophecy was not from God. A message promised protection in the temple but was instead a plot of reproach. *"Then I perceived that God had not sent him ... Tobias and Sanballat had hired him ... that I should be afraid and act that way and sin ... that they might reproach me."*[14]

When you pray more, you get closer to God and better understand that "if God be for me, no one can be against me."[15]

In dealing with the enemy, we are exhorted to be subtle as serpents and innocent as doves. By prayer, evil plots are aborted, strongholds are pulled down, enemies are disarmed and disasters averted. The enemy once attacked my dad's health, desiring his premature death, but it was revealed, and I aborted it in the spirit, by prayer.

> *"Indeed, prayer causes more coincidence than we can imagine. The power of prayer breaks all protocol."*

While at an evening service one day, my sister was admitted to a hospital several miles away. The *evil* plan was revealed to me, and she got deliverance through our intercession. My point is *evil plans* precede *actual physical attacks*. By prayer, a plan *is known* and the necessary spiritual action taken to combat it.

There is a thin line between the spiritual and physical. Those in the spirit see what happens in both worlds, but those in the flesh only see things in the physical world. Prayer is the bridge between the two and gives you a preview of happenings. You too can enjoy this golden advantage; pray to become spiritually sensitive.

An encounter at school is worth sharing. After I wrote an exam, I went out to pray to cancel all of Satan's plans. Some friends later found me and said the authorities wanted me. My exam paper was found 30 minutes after the expiration. They believed it was a calculated plan by the finder and me, and the supervisor denied seeing it. Though my paper had to be annulled, by my prayers, I was exempted. *Prayer miracles* save us greatly: a clear consequence was averted. Or was it a coincidence?

I *know* my family is *still intact* because of consistent prayers and God's mercies. I am deeply persuaded of the power of prayer, and I cannot afford to cease praying. Be watchful and vigilant: watch, pray always and avoid evil plots. Get praying, and soon you will *see* these results I testify of, and more.

Prayer births Confidence

Fearful and cowardly disciples who scattered when their master was arrested had the confidence to testify of Him boldly, *after* the upper room prayer experience.

As a saint of God, the more I pray, the more my confidence rises. Cowardice and shyness that kept me from public speaking gave way to inner and outward boldness: when I began to pray.

How do you get close to God's throne if not by prayer? Whenever the apostles and disciples were in trouble, they prayed: *Now LORD, look on their threats, and grant your servants that with all boldness they may speak your word, by stretching out your hand to heal, and that signs and wonders may be done through the name of ... Jesus ... and when they had prayed ... they were all filled with the Holy Spirit and spoke the word of God with boldness.*[16]

I assign prayer to where I cannot be, and the results are always amazing. A prayerful saint hardly quits in defeat. Do not toy with prayer, be confident, and pray with all sincerity and seriousness: get **praying now**!

Summary:

- Prayer gives meaning to realities before they happen.
- Prayer makes you see clearer and beyond your human reach.
- A praying man is stable, knows what's up and is *aware* of many events.
- Until you pray aright, you could be a beggar and never 'to the max.'
- Prayer awakens in us our hidden man and greatest potential.
- A praying man accesses God's throne and receives answers.

" THE MORE YOU PRAY IN THE SPIRIT, THE BETTER YOU UNDERSTAND THE OPERATIONS OF THE HOLY SPIRIT. "

CHAPTER SIX

PRAYING ALWAYS

I am always delighted to stay in the praying mood.

"If anyone asked me what is the first truly great secret of a successful prayer life, I would say in answer, praying in the Spirit." – *Saint Samuel Chadwick*

When I was younger, I least understood 'pray without ceasing.' It is still sensitive and debatable, with several schools of thought on how realistic it is. Many books share a lot, but Paul's teaching is simple and doable. '**I will pray *with* the spirit, and I will also pray with the understanding** (mind). **I will sing with the spirit and I will also sing *with* the understanding** (mind).'[1]

Praying with your mind

Praying with your understanding is when your mind is fruitful in a known dialect, and your hearers are fully *aware* of your speech. You are specific in your request, using a common language. It is fruitless to pray with the spirit language when making confessions: using the plain words of your dialect *is* more appropriate and potent.

To sum up prayers in a gathering, a dialect is suitable for hearers to respond in order. Praying in the Spirit could be fruitless when we know not what is being said: saying 'Amen' is hard and perhaps meaningless.

It is important to be fruitful in your mind to concentrate on what you are praying (saying). Making a request requires being fruitful in your thoughts about your exact need so as to pray with meaning. "To pray correctly, you must be mentally alert and vigilant." – *Dr. Curtis Mitchell, Biola College.*

Praying with your mind is limiting. You cannot do that for long without getting repetitive and bored. Yet, your mind focuses on hitting the target without wasting punches. This is useful in confession, declaration, deliverance, request and warfare.

> *"All God's saints must yearn to be in His presence in prayer so that we can demonstrate His power."*

Singing with your mind makes you ponder and reflect on the words, focus on its implication and thus be exhorted. In a gathering, it is effective and proper to pray and sing in understanding. Although, it is possible to speak in diverse tongues to convey a message to all hearers, as happened on the day of Pentecost. They spoke in tongues, yet the gathering, from different nations, could hear them telling the mighty works of God in their own specific dialects.[2]

Sensitive to his hearers, Jesus often prayed with the mind: *"Father ... I know You always hear me, but because of the people standing by I said this, that they may believe you have sent me."*[3]

Praying in the Spirit

Praying 'in the Spirit' or 'with the Spirit' is when saints speak in an unknown language, commonly described as speaking in tongues, a gift of the Holy Spirit, which enables you to pray rightly and for long. The world cannot comprehend this as they know not the Holy Spirit. *'They were all filled with the Holy Spirit and began to speak with other tongues, as the Spirit gave them utterance.*

'For he who speaks in a tongue does not speak to men but to God, for no one understands him; however, in the spirit he speaks mysteries.'[4]

"Praying in the Spirit gives the believer the opportunity to share secrets with God which prevents eavesdropping by others." – **The Holy Spirit, my Senior Partner**, Yonggi Cho.

The evidence of this remarkable gift inaugurated the early church and equipped her with power. The observing multitudes found it awesome. "*Human wisdom and desires can achieve human results but praying in the Spirit produces divine results.*" – Anon

Speaking in tongues edifies the individual; while diverse kinds of tongues edify the church, along with the gift of interpretation of tongues for the benefit of hearers. When the Holy Spirit has come on you, it is a great experience to pray in the Spirit.[5]

Larry Lea, in *The Joy of Prayer*: "*It is possible to obey Paul's command to pray in the Spirit on all occasions. The only way to pray on all occasions and continually is to pray in the Spirit. As you do so, the Holy Spirit comes to your aid, joins his strong supplication with yours and intercedes before God, enabling you to pray according to the perfect will of God ... Your spirit has access to your vocal cords just as your mind ... Therefore by your will, a prayer made in a praying language can come out of your spirit, bypass your mind, go over your tongue and go straight to God."*[6]

Praying in the Spirit is like projecting a laser beam that pierces through the enemy's territory and reaches God for immediate response. It helps you to have a constant attitude of prayer, regardless of activity or place. Only God receives the mysteries you utter in the Spirit.

I love praying in the Spirit very often: speaking mysteries to God without human meddling. It edifies my spirit and encourages me to pray more. My personal experience confirms Saint Samuel Chadwick's: *"praying with the Spirit is the key to my life; it awakes my mind and my heart. It gave me a new bible and a new message. Above all it gave me a new understanding and intimacy in the communion and ministry of prayer, it taught me to pray in the Spirit."*

The more you pray in the Spirit, the better you understand the operations of the Holy Spirit, to give Him a chance to complete His work in you. *"Whenever you come together, each of you has a psalm, has a teaching, has a tongue, has a revelation, has an interpretation. Let all things be done for edification."*[7]

Speaking in tongues is for all saints, not just for a few privileged. The *gift* is still evident in the church. I have experienced the perfect workings of these three gifts – speaking in tongues, diverse kinds of tongues and interpretation of tongues. All can operate in one person for edifying an individual and the church. I pray with the spirit in order to experience more of such an awesome display of power. You can use the spirit language to prophesy, and another will receive the understanding and interpret it for the benefit of a gathering.

Praying without Ceasing

"With my eyes closed?" I initially found it absurd till I learned that Yeshua said so, and Paul practiced and advised the same. I then studied to grasp how to develop an attitude of praying always and also discovered several forms of prayer that enable us to pray without ceasing.

Men always ought to pray and not to lose heart ... praying always with all prayer and supplication in the Spirit, being watchful to this end with all perseverance and supplication for all the saints ... pray without ceasing.[8]

Praying without ceasing *is being* conscious of God's presence and actually *staying* in His presence *always*. It is not about having your eyes closed but being in a praying mood *always*. When fully conscious of God's presence all day and night, the communion does *not* cease.

Prayer is integral in a Christian's life and should be continual. The miraculous work of regular prayer possesses and re-shapes every area of your life. You discipline and tune your spirit to an endless frequency modulation of prayer, which quickens and motivates body and soul. '*God is Spirit, and those who worship Him must do so in spirit and truth.*' When you believe this, prayer is not a mere activity but your nature, lifestyle and attitude.[9]

It is possible to pray always with your mind and spirit by adopting a disciplined attitude and maintaining a praying mood and steadily training your sub-conscience to grasp this.

"The more you pray in the Spirit, the better you understand the operations of the Holy Spirit."

Paul taught several forms of prayer to be in constant touch and in tune with God. The act of worship is prayer and vice versa. Meditating and singing hymns amounts to prayer. Prayer is an all-around attitude that involves your whole being. It is said that "anything that establishes a relationship between us and God is a form of prayer." Speaking to one another *in psalms and hymns and spiritual songs, singing and making melody in your heart to the LORD.*[10]

You can enjoy singing spiritual songs when you pray more. At certain times, you may not be able to utter words like Hannah: *"As she continued praying before the LORD ... Hannah spoke in her heart; only her lips moved but her voice was not heard."*[11]

You can pray *anywhere* and do other things at the same time. I often pray when working, whether alone or with people around. That way I *flow* with the Spirit and remain in tune for His directions. I even pray for persons I am talking with. I wake up from bed praying as if I was continuing from when I slept, and the results are marvelous. You *can* experience this prayer attitude.

I discovered three kinds of prayer. The first is where you are obliged to pray for a *request* or a *need* at a gathering. You would pray thus when you are asked to ('no need, no prayer'). Some Christians *only* pray when they want God's attention for their difficulties but would abandon prayer when all seems fine and okay.

The second is where you pray with *time*, guided by the clock. You finish praying when the time is up. On the Mount of Olives, He found His disciples sleeping because they finished praying. *'So you could not pray with me for an hour?'* And then He went back again to pray. Prayer should not end when the appointed meeting is over or when we sleep. Do you pray for an hour? We *believe* Jesus meant praying for an hour is the ideal *minimum*. It seems long, but when you develop a prayer attitude, 'praying without ceasing' becomes essential.

The third kind is *getting lost in His presence*; where your spirit contacts and interacts with divinity and you desire to *remain* there forever. Time is of no essence. A similar thing occurs in the occult world where they can travel in spirit, but *we enter* God's presence and remain there for days. His grace enables us to pray always.

It is worth praying for several hours.

Not so much the hours in praying but really enjoying His presence and glory like the three disciples who witnessed Jesus transfigured on the mount. Prayer ushers us into God's presence. We must daily maintain this attitude as our prayer character.

God's Generals of old developed prayer character and attitude and had such testimonies. William Bramwell, a Welsh preacher, once spent 36 hours in a sand pit alone praying. Mountains and woods have been ideal *venues* for God's Generals to pray. A present-day General, spends 12 hours saying 'good morning, God' just to enjoy His presence.

"One hour with God infinitely exceeds all the pleasures and delights of this lower world." – *David Brainerd*

"I have learned that greater things could only be wrought by daily contact with God than by preaching." – *Billy Graham*

I see why Moses stayed so long on Mount Sinai and why he was an able leader, always engulfed in God's presence. The more we pray, the deeper the intimacy between God and us.

All God's saints must yearn to be in His presence in prayer so that we can demonstrate His power. Do not just *reach* His gates, *enter* into His courts (presence). I had an amazing experience on my 18th birthday when we went to pray in the woods for several days. When we returned, the anointing was so strong people could hardly look at our faces, and we had great favor. The Spirit's presence was strong, and we helped many people overcome their spiritual problems. Incredibly, some could not look into our eyes, and some fell before us because of the anointing.

I just want to be where you are, dwelling daily in your presence ♪.
I don't want to worship from afar, draw me near to where you are ♫.
I want to be where you are, dwelling in your presence, feasting at your table, surrounded by your glory.
In your presence, that is where I always want to be ...
I just want to be with you." – **Don Moen**

Reaching this level and achieving this attitude has been a great journey of great discipline. I get excited in God's presence, and I desire to stay *there* forever. I get needs met when I pray, but my greatest desire is a non-stop stay in His presence. Faint not; give prayer no holiday.

Summary:

- Praying with understanding is necessary and effective.
- Praying in the Spirit edifies your spirit and quickens your sensitivity.
- Praying always is an acquired attitude, developed and sustained for life.
- Prayer is not minutes, hours or days but a lifestyle.
- Worship, praise and prayer are attitudes not determined by meetings and rhythms.

"A PRAYER LIFE BACKED BY FASTING UNEARTHS SPIRITUAL POTENTIAL FOR DREAMS AND VISIONS TO MATERIALIZE."

CHAPTER SEVEN

PRAYER 'AIDS'

"Praying is work. Taxing work with tireless and endless toil. It is no easy road ... there is no easy path to glory, and there is no easy road to fame. Prayer, no matter how you view it is no simple parlour game. But its prizes call for fighting."
– Dick Eastman, No Easy Road

Prayer is a multichannel road to one destination: a combination of certain spiritual exercises and virtues for certain guaranteed results. Prayer is indeed a hard road of persistent battles before a prize *is* obtained. The other exercises and virtues alongside prayer become very potent and are thus essential for going beyond our reach.

"A prayer life backed by fasting unearths spiritual potential for dreams and visions to materialize."

People who led exemplary lives in dedication to God are deemed as spiritual pillars beyond earthly limits. Jesus severally exhorted us to live by these virtues to excel in our generation. For awesome successes and abundant blessing, let us examine the spiritual significance of these **four** essential **'F'**s.

Fasting

Whole books convey its full spiritual significance. Many are the rewards and victories of fasting. This principle still *works*: 'it pays to pay a prize for victory.'

Fasting is not a pre-requisite to move God's hand but a surrender of self and a display of dependence on God. When you *humble* yourself with a fast, you subject your body to sobriety and deny your flesh of food and pleasures. Your spirit is fortified by a purposeful fast. You then become better positioned to receive spiritual direction. You will endure self-denial for a while, but it is a very profitable spiritual exercise.

Fasting provides an upper-hand over spiritual hosts of wickedness and sensitizes you to be more effective in your spiritual relationship with God. It empowers you and provides the gift of discernment of spirits.

Fasting endues you with awesome power as God compensates you for His mission. Where we place God determines the success or otherwise of any ministry.

"*And Jesus, being filled with the Holy Spirit ... being tempted for 40 days by the devil ... he ate nothing.*" At the beginning of his ministry, Jesus fasted for 40 days. The *master* fasted for a spiritual awakening, how much more should we, his disciples?[1]

A Spirit-filled saint appreciates the necessity of fasting as a good and profitable exercise, an action to stand against militating forces. When we fast, we humble our flesh and engulf it with the power of the Holy Spirit. Fasting and prayer could facilitate receiving God's direction.

Ezra and Esther proclaimed and led their people to fast: 'that we might afflict ourselves ... to seek God for a right way for us and our goods ... so we fasted, and God listened to our entreaty. She said: 'gather together all God's people ... and fast for me.'[2]

Fasting is a sign of total surrender to God. It helps in repenting from sin as the people of Nineveh did. Fasting indicates remorse and change of attitude to *return* to God.

Moses fasted, so did David and his men, Daniel and his friends in Babylon and Paul and his team, to mention a few.

Important Note: You can only achieve certain victories by combining fasting and prayer. Jesus emphasized the need for fasting when He, the bridegroom, is no more with us in the flesh. Include a fast in your fervent prayer for far-reaching results. His strength is made perfect in our weakness.[3]

Fasting has many advantages. It is recommended in medicine among other therapies for detoxification. Studies indicate that fasting enables some enzymes to work optimally, and as you drink more water, unwanted materials are ejected. Also, the body is forced to use stored fat as food, thus reducing the risk of some medical conditions.

Many saints are overwhelmed with the cares and burdens of life: the weights of sin, idleness, indiscipline, inconsistent devotion, etc. A good dose of fasting is good for us to remain *in line*. Intense fasting and prayer based on the WORD make us sensitive to the Holy Spirit. Replace worrying with regular fasting and prayer. However, without the WORD, prayer and fasting *become* starving.

When a fast is proclaimed, spend much time praying to benefit fully spiritually as intense hunger will follow. I used not to, but I have learned to fast, and I concentrate better when fasting. The more I deny my body of food, the more my spirit awakens to spiritual things. Fasting is quite taxing, but you cannot underestimate it: you reach higher grounds in the spirit realm—which will actualize in the physical. Learn how to fast.[4]

Faith

"**Now the just shall live by faith.**" Faith is a highly recommended virtue that aids prayer. By faith, a saint's life is well lived and is victorious indeed.[5]

Faith involves belief and trust and translates the unseen into realities. Faith is 'the substance of things hoped for, the evidence of things not seen' (you can feel a substance). By faith, any image can be real, substantial, evidential and definite and could appear. Faith cancels the natural laws of *seeing to believe*.

Without faith, it is impossible to please God. You must believe He exists and He rewards those who diligently seek Him. The appreciation of the existence of the *Godhead* becomes real by faith. Prayer gives breath to faith to give birth to expression. Prayer and faith coexist for a greater effect, fueling belief and trust in the faithfulness of God to make all things possible. Prayer strengthens faith to enable us to see things from God's viewpoint. Faith brings God's WORD into existence. Prayer cancels doubt and fear to help faith grow. When I look at the physical, I see challenges, but when I tarry in prayer, I see visions fulfilled.[6]

Faith comes from the WORD. A seed is sown when you hear the WORD, and it generates your faith in God's abilities. You can gain faith in the integrity of God's WORD. I asked God in prayer one day: 'when shall these things happen?' **"I AM faithful to do what I will do for My name's sake,"** He answered. Truly, 'faith is words confessed until they are possessed.' Abraham did that and was enabled to hold on to God's promises.[7]

Prayer and faith combined kicks out failure and uncertainties and propels you into the future with great assurances, presenting a stepping-stone unto better platforms. Prayer and faith access your deliverance and stores treasures for your future use. The working of your faith translates spoken and written words into reality.

Mary believed the angel's word: "nothing is impossible with God." 'I am the Lord's handmaid, be it unto me according to your word.'

There come times of utter hopelessness, considering your family situation and competition all around you. I get discouraged too, but I am reinforced in prayer, believing that God is able. Prayer strengthens my weak faith, and I hope and hold His promises for my life. Life is uncertain, but the integrity of the WORD builds our faith in His faithfulness, knowing that what He has said will surely be manifested.[8]

God is faithful *always*. We must reach the point of being fully persuaded that He will do exactly what He says. I love most to use this quote in prayer: "LORD you said to me, *'thou hast well seen; for I will hasten my WORD to perform it.'*"9KJV

At times we experience unstableness concerning our promises. Quit doubting and fit yourself into God's vision. Have resolute faith that God can do it because double-mindedness can deny God's blessing.10

By faith, I prayed for my mum, and she *avoided* a planned surgery as suggested by a physician. By the prayer of faith, I have lived ill-free for many years. When once I was diagnosed with malaria, I *launched* into prayer and asked God to "give me fresh blood from the stripes of Jesus." A new test at the hospital the next day showed no trace of malaria parasites.

> **"If you have faith as a mustard seed,**
> **you will say to this mountain, 'move from here to there,'**
> **and it will; and nothing will be impossible for you ...**
> **the apostles said to the Lord, 'increase our faith.'"11**

By faith, the disciples lived with varying degrees of miracles and healings and received good reports even in death. By faith, they overcame many odds and obstacles. 12

I once prayed for a four-year-old who had never walked, whose younger sister had started walking. His mom had done all she could. Nothing happened instantly, but I was convinced of a miracle. The next day, he held onto walls and took his first steps. Prayer of faith birthed a miracle for a child.

Fearlessness

For God has not given us a spirit of fear, but of power and of love and of a sound mind.[13]

Satan's stronghold on Christians is fear. Fear, which associates with failure and doubt, stirs our emotions, dominates our minds and impresses that either 'God cannot do it' or 'we do not deserve it.' Many times, the WORD boldly exhorts us: "Fear not." As Christians, we *have* power over fear, and we must repeatedly profess His WORD with faith. *"O LORD, because you are with me, I will not fear."* [14]

"Much prayer, much power" is a certain saying. Where does this power come from? Prayer increases confidence in God, which loses the grip of the fear latched on our minds. The more you pray, the greater your capacity to overcome fear. Fear thwarts your efforts, but you can quench it with fervent prayer.

When they had received power in the Holy Spirit, the once faithless and fearful disciples boldly burst out testifying about Jesus the Messiah. Whenever they faced difficulty, they prayed earnestly for strength to forge ahead with the gospel in great confidence. They were fearless even in persecutions and death. They were filled with power in demonstrating what Christ bequeath to them: the Holy Spirit.[15]

Consider the fearless nature of people Daniel, David, Deborah, Nehemiah, Paul and others. Their sincere faith in the power of prayer made them stronger and bolder to face their challenges. They were prayerful, fearless and full of faith. Whenever I pray, my fears give way to faith, which increases my boldness.

"Do not let fear freeze you, let faith free you."

Fear kills slowly. Satan uses fear as a weapon to intimidate God's saints and ultimately 'kill' them. Fear grips, limits and destroys lives, killing many prematurely. Fear breeds anxiety and worry possesses you and re-directs your focus.

When fear lasts to influence your core, you become preoccupied with it. When that happens, many ills also follow suit.

Satan fires arrows of fear to replace faith in God to thwart your purpose in life. Child of God, do not sign the covenant of fear drafted by Satan. Three hundred sixty-five times, His WORD exhorts "Fear not" (one dose per day).

Favor

Favor endues praying saints with testimonies. God's favor brings and causes some people to work *for* us.

When you are favored of God, you *will* receive favor from men. We have come this far in life and our faith walk because of God's favor. **And Jesus increased in wisdom and stature, and in favor with God and men.** [16]

God's favor opens doors of opportunity, and we gain *things* we would otherwise never have obtained. This kindness of God brings awesome miracles and propels us unto greater heights.

Times are tough, and they are coupled with unfair *universal* competition. Nepotism and favoritism rule in all circles: social, political, economic. If you *know nobody*, you have no connection, no job or contract, no income and you have no life. Only a few have privileges. *Moving forward* is tough. Our world and age *are* saturated with many inhibitions that make survival hard.

It is so hard to be successful in any sphere of life. Many achieve success on the backs of parents and or powerful officials. Things are easy for some who do not have to wait for long. For the majority, life is a daily struggle to reach the top: every day is a fight for survival.

In comes God's divine favor, to fulfill all dreams. God's favor has brought me thus far. Some great friends of mine, to mention a few, Ebenezer Nana Anti, Mr. and Mrs. Eric Owusu Agyeman, prophet Samuel Fosu and Jerry Bentil *agree* with me that we have come so far on praying knees, that God's favor and mercies continuously aided and rightly connected us, paving the way for all that we have, which *were* initially unimaginable.

"Whoever the Lord knows and favors, greatly excels!"

Esther, a Hebrew orphan and captive, was favored in a foreign land. She became queen and later played a major role in delivering her people from a planned genocide. When *they all* fasted and prayed, the beloved Esther found favor before the king of Persia.[17]

Joseph found favor as a slave in Egypt. In Potiphar's house, he was elevated to chief servant. Later as a prisoner he was elevated to chief warden and finally was elevated second to Pharaoh, to secure Egypt's well-being and survival. In captivity, Daniel and his friends had favor before the king's eunuch— above those selected to serve Babylon's king.[18]

David's life is a fine example of divine favor: from a shepherd boy in the bush to serving the king and finally made king of Israel. God favored David when He sent Samuel to anoint him king in place of King Saul, whom God had rejected. Clearly, God's favor endeared David to Prince Jonathan to so love him to the point of severally saving David from King Saul's death sentence.[19]

Considering these accounts and mine, I *know* God's favor is real. No matter how much you pray, be sure to bask in the four virtues: fasting, faith, fearlessness and favor, which are proven and effective aids for 'mountain-moving' prayers.

> *"When God is involved, all protocol is broken."*

I so cherish the FAVOR of God. Though young, I have come quite far in my life. By prayer and divine favor, my life has improved from grace to grace: through my schooling, professional course, work experience and employment to a most fruitful marriage, priestly ministry and other areas of my life.

To move further on to higher grounds and greater success, I will pray always and bask in divine favor. Be a candidate of His favor too. You know what to do.

Summary:

- Fasting benefits spiritually and physically, an advantage to those who pray with purpose.
- Faith sees what God sees, believes what He knows and confesses them till they come to pass.
- The antidote to fear is faith: 'greater is He in us than he that is in the world.'
- Favor bypasses protocol and births opportunities, and with divine mercy, manifests God's promises.

LET YOUR LIGHT SO SHINE
BEFORE MEN, THAT THEY
MAY SEE YOUR GOOD WORKS
AND GLORIFY YOUR FATHER
IN HEAVEN.

>─┤ CHAPTER EIGHT ├─←

BE HOLY

**"Pursue after Holiness, press towards this blessed mark,
let your thirsty soul continually say, I shall never be satisfied
till I awake in thy kindness."** – *David Brainerd*

Holiness *amounts* to prayer. Your body serves as the 'living sacrifice unto God.' This blessed standard cannot be ignored or overemphasized.[1]

**"Pursue peace with all people, and holiness,
without which no one will see the LORD."**

You can *choose* to *disbelieve* God and remain a *failure*, but holiness should never be compromised if you desire to *see* God. His kingdom is not food and drink, but righteousness, peace and joy in the Spirit ... pursue holiness; else you cannot see God.[2]

The church is full of Christians with questionable lifestyles; hence many prayers go unanswered. They *have* charisma without godliness and shamelessly live in sin yet are often seen praising God, fooling themselves. Is it any wonder why God seems so far away when the church gathers? Because God hates sin, which separates us from Him, we mostly miss the awesome presence of the Spirit.[3]

"Be holy, for I am holy." Holiness is God's standard for living; He strictly requires an uncompromised holy life if we desire to see Him. God sent Jesus to exchange our rottenness for *His* righteousness so we can become His children. Holiness is crucial to a saint's life and walk; it is the nature that *hallows* God in us, wherever we are.[4]

Inherent character

Just as he who called you is holy, be holy in all your conduct. If you are *born again*, you become God's child and He, your Father. You must obey Him, imbue godly character in you, live a life of holiness and thus become the light and salt of your world because He *lives* in you. You are His *adoption*, to demonstrate His righteousness, that *He lives in you* indeed.[5]

I get chills at *how* some supposed Christians are comfortably immoral and yet claim God's adoption. Fornication *seems* normal among God's people, now but holiness is crystal-clear and pure without stain, spot or blemish. That is the life God wants us to demonstrate.

> *"Let your light so shine before men, that they may see your good works and glorify your Father in heaven."*[6]

We can attain God's measure of holiness if we let *in* His Spirit and bear His fruit.[7]

Everyone experiences that peculiar new life sensation when you first receive, accept and confess Jesus as your Lord and personal savior. That *enables* you to live a life of holiness because we are called to be holy. Be sure to *add* holiness to the call to pray; live a holy life.[8]

A sacrifice

The priest himself must be sanctified (holy) to enter the temple's chamber to intercede; else he could be stricken to death. You are a *royal priesthood,* and I implore you to present your body a living sacrifice, holy and acceptable unto God as your spiritual worship.[1]

You may devote your time and money to the poor, but without holiness, you will not see God. You are *born again,* not to some religion but to the *life of God.* He *gave* His only begotten Son and His Spirit so that we will *know* who God the Father is, so that we too can *worship* Him.[9]

Ultimately, God sacrificed His only begotten son to reconcile us to Himself, to live a *life* that pleases Him. God loves absolute purity and desires the best of our lives as a sacrifice.

> *"You may devote your time and money to the poor, but without holiness, you will not see God."*

The church swims in a creeping sin of compromise. Worldliness and double standards have overtaken God's church, vexing righteous saints with worldly holiness. Advanced technology and heightened media sex-appeal have made abominations normal. Attraction to sin is common as the world sets standards for the church. Every imaginable sin is *in* today's church. *For that righteous man dwelling among them tormented his righteous soul from day to day by seeing and hearing their lawless deeds.*[10]

It is fashionable to be a church member and still serve mammon. Many disregard the virtue of holiness and have sold their 'birthright' for mere fleshly pleasure.[11]

Many consciences are seared as with hot iron, and they feel no guilt for wrongdoings. They live in sin and still belong to the church. They ENTER and EXIT sin as they would a shopping mall. Righteousness exhortations abound, but they care less for holiness. Virginity is sacrificed for bread, and it is *hard* to tell worldly people apart from God's saints.

Where are the 'Josephs,' 'Daniels,' 'Josiahs,' Japheth's 'daughters,' the 400 daughters of Benjamin, the two virgins in Sodom and Gomorrah and the wise virgins?

God counts on your righteousness and holiness to move in our midst. The fervent prayer of the righteous has great power in its effects. Holiness speaks and can complement our prayers effectively. His coming is near; be holy.[12]

Summary:

- Holiness is a prayer providing an opportunity to sacrifice yourself to God.
- You can *avoid* faith, but without holiness, you cannot see God.
- Your holiness is an appreciation for the ultimate sacrifice on the tree for your sins.
- No matter how evil the world gets, God has a holy and righteous remnant. Join now while there is room.

"BE STILL"

When you're still, you dialogue with God in meditation, and you appreciate better your relationship with Him. You avoid interruption to have the prospect to *hear* from God: a period to calm all conflicts in your spirit and soul, a quiet time in a solitary place to commune with Him. It is essential in a dialogue (prayer) to hear God speak also. We miss this when we rush off after praying.

Prayer establishes a relationship between God our Father and us His children. His *hotline* is always *receiving* our calls (prayer). He never hangs up and is never too busy to attend to callers. However, we deny God His right to respond: because we rush in prayer and rush out afterward. We do that and fail to hear His response.

God's direct hotline is **OT.MP.JER33:3 (Old Testament, Major Prophet, Jeremiah 33:3):** "*Call to me, and I will answer you and show you great and mighty things, which you do not know.*" This verse affirms His desire to hear you pray always and for Him to respond accordingly: the only barrier being our sin. "If I regard iniquity in my heart, the LORD will not hear me ... He has not turned away His mercy from me."[1]

Knowing that He answers us, we must learn *how to be still*. One of the several ways is to point out a portion of His WORD and impress it upon our spirit as He speaks mostly through the Bible. Through prayer, God might *lead* you to read certain Bible verses to answer your supplications.

Again, learn to identify His still small voice. 'Be still' and hear God addressing your situation.[2]

In **The hour that changes the world**, Dick Eastman shares experiences in prayer and the need to develop meditation. Individuals should cultivate the habit of waiting upon God patiently after prayer to hear His voice, describing it as being spiritually and mentally alert (sensitive) to God's Spirit.

I enjoy most the state of stillness away from any disturbance as I focus on receiving *direction* and insight from God. Fear not, stand still and see His salvation.[3]

Much stress and depression make it difficult to *hear* God. At the Red Sea, instead of listening for direction, the Israelites accused their leaders of 'bringing us here to die.' They paid more attention to their situation than what God would do. We also focus more on the cares of life and thus magnify our problems to seem bigger than God. When they were still, God directed Moses in how to cross the sea on dry ground. God never fails: keep still and let Him.

"Indeed, God speaks, sometimes with the 'still small voice.'"[4]

If you can still your emotions in turbulent situations and pray, God will show you what to do. We pray because we need His direction, guide and daily provision; how can you ignore God's answer to your cries if you must prosper in all you do?

I claim no intense experiences, but God speaks to me severally in diverse ways; at times He speaks directly to my spirit. I recall a particular *bathroom experience* at age 15 when God *showed* me His purpose for my life. I wrote several articles years back when He asked me to write down things He would show me so I could edify the church. I least knew where He was taking me, but I am a living testimony, and God is still using me.

What He showed me years ago are actualizing now. Many Christians do hear from God in our generation. He spoke to many Patriarchs ages ago: He still speaks, in His still small voice. It is amazing how I *hear* God, but I do know when He speaks. Individuals hear God differently. How do we identify God's voice? His Spirit *touches* our spirit to *know* He is speaking, especially when you *are* holy.

Once God has spoken...

Twice have I heard this, that power belongs to Him. David often 'inquired of the LORD' through priests and prophets: he and God often communed with each other. David worshipped God, and God loved him for his reverence. The LORD gives three *general* answers: 'Yes,' 'No,' 'Wait.'[5]

"YES"

Because there is a need and yes will do a lot of good. Our heavenly Father knows our needs before we ask him, and He gives only what is best. Yes from God is affirmative, and we receive instant answers. For some requests, it does not take long for me to receive answers. For some, God releases answers right when I pray.[6]

With a day left to close High School exam registration, in very hard times, I was sent home for the fees, ¢40,000.00 then (now GH¢4.00). We could *only* pray for a solution, and as we did, a family friend visited and just gave us the exact amount. I thank God for many such cases.

Just as He gives to me when in need, I have learned to give to God when He asks anything of me. He will not ask for what I cannot offer.

George Mueller's instant answer to his prayer: he needed money for a trip, and he so *believed* God would provide. Two people before his turn at the ticket booth, the man ahead left the queue, handing him the amount he needed. Our Father is a *crucial-point-of-need* God. He delights in our prayers: 'ask, and you will receive, that your joy may be full.'[7]

"NO"

God's NO is not a negative response or a denial of your request. The *all-knowing* God always has the best for you at the right time. His NO is in your best interest, probably meant to save you from looming danger. You ask for *many* things, but you least know their consequence. Beware: your *urgent* requests may lead to *ruin*. Though it may seem right, its end could be *death*.[8]

If you who are *corrupt*, give good gifts to your children, how much more will your Father in heaven give you good things? Good because every good and perfect gift is from God.[9]

I receive many NOs too, and I get discouraged. In my ignorance, I sometimes question God, but with time, I appreciate why God said no. He meets our needs according to His riches in glory. I made a particular request several times, and God always said no.

David once desired to pursue enemies who had raided his camp, but God said NO. Learn to understand God's NO to avoid His displeasure. You could get your request *plus* sorrows if you *insist* God should grant it. Please learn from Balaam, who nearly got killed for overriding God's NO.[10]

Demons can *withhold* your answers, and you may think God said NO. The 'Prince of Persia' *detained* Daniel's answer, and that is why we must be in the spirit to know if God says NO or if an enemy is hindering our requests.[11]

"WAIT"

Wait is an important vocabulary word in our relationship with God, but we are too often in a hurry to **WAIT**. In our walk with God, praying teaches us to wait on God, and patience is a virtue and fruit of the Holy Spirit in us.

WAIT! God *is* preparing your request for the right time as a good gift. Probably, your raw request needs processing, or He has to first sieve out the danger from your request. Our *ways* are not the ways of the LORD.[12]

"Learn to understand God's NO to avoid His displeasure."

We will slowly grasp this. God may be training and equipping you to handle your requests better when they arrive, so they will not destroy you. If you do not mature enough, your request will be denied. To *be* a mighty warrior, David trained in the bush; he fought a lion and a bear before defeating Goliath. Moses trained many years in the wilderness for the Exodus. Joseph trained in many situations for his youthful dreams to actualize. Do not run ahead of God's schedule for your life (in your requests). While you wait, God prepares His intended gifts for you.

For a particular opening, He asked me to wait, and I did for many years while still praying until the answer dropped. I am *still expecting some* answers, and I know God will respond positively; He always does. "Wait patiently for the Lord; He will hearken to your prayers."

Waiting has no time: just be patient. Do not be robbed of the opportunity to appreciate God's intents. Abraham waited twenty-five years to *see* his promised child. How long have you waited? Have assurance in God and wait. *If it seems slow, wait for it ... it will surely come.*[13]

In answer to our prayers, either a 'Yes,' 'No' or 'Wait' is a good, perfect and positive answer from God: but be more interested in God's direction. Learn to hear Him speak and be familiar with His answers.

Summary:
- Every message has a response. God definitely responds to prayer.
- Learning to hear Him is as essential as praying to God.
- Despise not the attitude to wait upon God patiently.

NEVER BOX GOD IN YOUR
EXPECTATIONS.
WE ARE HUMAN
AND LIMITED ...
HE IS OMNISCIENT
AND OMNIPOTENT.

CHAPTER TEN

GOD'S SOVEREIGNTY

It is obvious, and there is no doubt about it at all, that all power *belongs* to God Almighty. [1]

Prayer is not only for spiritual battles but also for knowing and relating to God personally. The destination of prayer is the Most High God, 'the Alpha and Omega.' An exposé on prayer is incomplete without *exposing* the glory and sovereignty of *Elohim, Elyon, Nissi, Shaddai, Shalom, Tsidkenu, Sabaoth,* etc. [2]

His *nature* is immutable. Only He **can** do what *should be* and not what we think is right. His *righteousness* sets the standard for the truth.

God fulfills what He says. **He "is not man that He should lie, nor a son of man, that He should repent. Has he said, and will He not do? Or has He spoken, and will He not make it good." [3]**

Humans doubt and question God when He answers prayer *by* His sovereign nature, which can never be altered even by our prayers. Since first publishing this book, I am daily learning to understand more of God's sovereignty.

"The best way to understand God is not to understand Him." – *Abraham Bioh, Alive Chapel, NY.*

We try to figure out God's answer to our prayers. Yes, we must 'ask, seek and knock,' but that cannot change how God, in His infinite wisdom, chooses to respond. *Even* Elijah missed God's visitation contrary to his expectations. God chose to come in "a still small voice" and not in the 'great and strong wind, earthquake or fire.' He is sovereign.[4]

Never *box* God in your expectations. Why *get* disappointed for not receiving answers according to your desires? Someone who once exclaimed to me: '*If God does not answer this prayer; I will stop serving Him.*' This frustration is *common*, but no one *threatens* God and succeeds. We *are human* and *limited*. **HE IS OMNISCIENT** and **OMNIPOTENT**.

Oh, how we used to make *childish prayer requests*. As a parent, I have learned that children are not aware of the implications of their many *wants*. Being limited in what we know, we should be thankful that God did not grant some of our requests. We must accept our Father's absolute rule in our lives.[5]

Do not confuse God's sovereignty when the enemy withheld Daniel's answer. He eventually received the answer because God is ABLE. "*for from the first day ... your words were heard ... but the prince of Persia withstood me twenty-one days and behold Michael ... came to help me.*" Knowing this, learn to pray all *manner* of prayers.[6]

God's sovereign election

"**JACOB I LOVED (chose, protected, blessed) BUT ESAU I HATED (held in disregard compared to Jacob).**" **AMP** [7]

We often *wonder* God's fairness in this situation. The apostle Paul sought to address it and concluded that it all stemmed from God's Sovereignty, not man's desire. God's choice depends not on human will or effort (the totality of human striving), but on who He chooses to show mercy (it is His sovereign gift).

"Never box God in your expectations.
We are human and limited but
He is omniscient and omnipotent."

As we try to understand His sovereignty here, let us ask some questions. What did Esau do before birth to merit God sidelining him? Did God really hate Esau; how would a merciful God do that? Does God show favoritism? Was there unrighteousness in Esau? Bang! That is it! His righteousness is His standard, so God never lied. **His WORD** and **ACTIONS** are the foundation upon which everything depends.

Jacob could pass for *worse* for tricking his older brother to *take* his birthright and for conniving with his mother to usurp Esau's blessing by pretending to be Esau. Why would God prefer a *deceiver*? God is the righteous judge. He *judges* our thoughts and hearts and *reviews* intents and purposes. More than *anything* we must *mind* what is in our hearts and thoughts.[8]

Comic illustration:

1st boy: "Oh God, please help us find our lost $20, and we will give you $10."

2nd boy: "How can you say that when the item we need costs exactly $20?"

1st boy: "I am using that to *bait* God for help; of course, we can't give him $10."

Can you imagine this? Mind your *intents* when you pray. You want a job, a baby, a car, a house, a travel opportunity, etc., so you often make vows for specific answers, yet you forget about the vows when the answers come. If God did not overlook our many errors, we all would have perished.

Esau never weighed the consequence of his decisions. He sought immediate gratification for his needs and lived a carefree life without much consideration. Esau decided to marry wives from unapproved tribes to displease his parents.

The omniscient God *knew* what would *be* if He had chosen Esau. So, in spite of Jacob's own flaw, he was preferred for his clean heart. *Hindsight* helps to review and learn from these Bible accounts, and God always *knows* the end from the beginning.

Never give up on God because of unanswered prayers or because your expectation was different. Instead, choose to submit to God's sovereignty. Learn to trust Him with perseverance and patience. You will soon understand why God does what He does even when we pray. Imagine perceiving someone who wrongs you as your enemy. You should learn to forgive rather than pray for God *to kill* your enemies. God cannot answer *such* prayers; else you too will soon die from someone's prayers.

Indeed, He *is* sovereign and will not answer selfish prayers. We desire and pray about certain things but then soon lost interest when we have them. We even blame God for the things we asked from Him. You wanted marriage, and now you are blaming and cursing everyone except yourself. Adam excused himself saying "it is the woman *you gave* me." You asked God for babies; why do you now complain of challenges in raising them? [9]

I *see* our ignorance in the many things we pray for, but for God's mercies (which are all in His sovereignty), we could be worse off.

Human nature is insatiable. We want rain, but soon we say, 'the rains are too much.' Though God responds when we call, He does not move as we wish when He knows the end is *bitter* or better.

Doubt not God's integrity: Job's case

The LORD answered Job ... who *is* this who darkens counsel by words without knowledge? Gird your loins like a man; for I will demand of you ... and answer me. Where were you when I laid the earth's foundations? Tell me, if you have understanding.[10]

Integrity is the state of being complete and undivided ... honest, trustworthy, upright, truthful, moral, righteous, etc. (*Encarta Dict.*). God's righteousness is His integrity. As you strive for integrity, know that it is the nature of God. 'I am the LORD and I do not change.'"

BEWARE: It is Satan's alpha-scheme to make us doubt and question God's integrity. So, we ask: "does God exist ... why do I *still* suffer ... why is He not bothered about my requests?" To worsen matters, we doubt God more when people around us seem to have explainable answers to *our* inexplicable situations. We tend to compare God to our human thinking and subject His ways to our questioning. Sometimes, you may justify why your prayers must be answered or why you must tell others that God disappointed you.

Upright Job feared God, but he went through a humongous trial. Nobody understood that Job was not the cause of what was happening to him. He *thought* he was 'perfect and upright' yet God was too far off to vindicate him.

When God finally came to answer Job's justification of righteousness and the misjudgment of Job's few friends, I thought Job would get direct answers to his many queries. Instead, everything said *addresses* God's majesty and sovereignty, of His creation and His command of nature. He affirmed: 'it is my right to choose and do what I want to do and no one can question me. I reserve the right. I am sovereign.'

I am convinced of God's sovereignty through and through. It is rather dangerous not to pray at all. People tell me that *when they start praying or being serious with the church, they experience challenges and attacks*. My response is: "If I pray for God's intervention and supernatural strength yet *these* things *happen*, what about when I do not pray at all ... my enemies would have a field day."

Be encouraged by this book: the greatest gift of communicating with your Father in heaven is through prayer. Share your faith, fears, pains and gains with Him in prayer. I did it by prayer, and so can you. God bless you.

Summary:
- Study God's Sovereignty in-depth (Romans 9:6-29).
- The nature of God makes Him immutable.
- Never box God in your expectations.
- God's righteousness is His integrity; never doubt Him.

CHAPTER ELEVEN

YOU CAN EXCEL

**"No one fails in prayer,
unless you fail to pray."**

With diligence, you can achieve anything you determine to do. You can excel in every area including your prayer life. God *made* us excellent, and none is born a failure, though success is the crown of hard work. If you decide to change your situation, you can excel too, if you commit to PRAYER.

Every stage in life has a *beginning*, so when you start, keep at it and never give up on praying.

Mind your priorities: regard prayer as your steering wheel and not a spare tire. You say "**I do not know how to pray, let alone excel in prayer**." Please be exhorted: Gideon thought of himself as "weak, least, incapable and was fearful but God called him a 'mighty man of valor.'"[1]

Do not block your breakthrough for miracles just because you will not pray. God's Spirit in you will *show* you to pray efficiently. You will learn how to pray as you *begin* to pray. "Prayer is an on-the-job exercise; you can only do it the hard way, by **PRAYING**." – *Ato Yawson*

You *can* excel in prayer and everything. Successful people *go* the extra mile and do not easily tire. They burn midnight candles to attain excellence. The lazy hardly try anything and give up easily, if they do try. The ordinary just settle for enough, when there *is* more. Those who go beyond ordinary receive more and excel, knowing there is always more. They *sacrifice* more time, work, study, money, prayer, etc., and they receive more, as desired.

'To him who has, more shall be given' and 'to who much is given, much is required.' The excellent do not get satisfied as we think they *should* be. Paul, the apostle, wrote: "I run forth with all perseverance to reach for the mark." If you do pray for 10 minutes only, boast not but take it higher to 20, 30 minutes and keep going.[2]

If you do one hour, you could increase it ... there is *more* ahead to conquer and achieve. Improve how you prayed yesterday: *someone* prays for twelve hours daily. "**GIVE US THIS DAY, OUR DAILY BREAD.**" It is not merely how long you pray but your daily attitude of discipline and consistency.

> **"Prayer is an on-the-job exercise; you can only
> do it the hard way, by PRAYING."** – *Ato Yawson*

Developing a prayer lifestyle is a hard task, needing discipline and resolve to devote yourself to prayer and not to give up in challenging times. You must defy all odds to achieve success: if you remain ordinary, you will *end* ordinary.

Prayer is never wasted, and no one fails in prayer. In the garden, they could hardly pray for one hour with their master, but they changed their destiny and developed a daily prayer attitude after *his ascension*.

If you are a very busy person, *let* prayer be inherent in your business. You could be so tired to want to set it aside, but never skip prayer. If you need God all the time, pray all the time, as much as humanly possible.

Prayer is not just for an hour or whatever period: it is important to develop an attitude of prayer for the whole day; it was a top priority in Jesus's ministry.

We need God more if we must prosper. Without God, we can achieve nothing, hence the need to stay in touch with Him in prayer.[3]

While working on this book, God *asked* me to pray for an hour a day apart from my usual appointment and church work. In addition to work, it was hard to pray more. Sometimes, I could not imagine myself doing one more hour after a hard day's work, but when I 'go and pray,' my joy and delight grow, and the results show. I receive fresh understanding and ideas to write what the elect of God should know.

Please note that lying in your bed to pray is suicide!

Many are known for what they do not practice. Not me. If we accept that prayer is breath to God's saints, then I will not stop breathing. Prayer has opened previously unimaginable great doors for me, and I hope to continue to excel. You too can excel.

*"I do not want to be called excellent.
I want to be found as one."*

Stop being a theologian of prayer who does not pray. Be a prayer practitioner: a **doer** and not just a preacher.

You needed to be encouraged. Be a doer. You can do it and achieve great success too. Stand and be counted, join God's end-time prayer army. He hears and answers the prayer of faith, according to His WORD and will. Prayer works! Pray without ceasing.

Summary:
- Prayer excellence is achievable if we task ourselves to pray.
- We must grow and increase what we do rather than grow cold.
- Failure is never the ultimate; it is a condition and not a state.
- You too can make it if you believe in yourself.

THE GREATEST PRAYER

Dear beloved, I invite you to pray the prayer of salvation now to be transformed from darkness into light after accepting Jesus Christ as your Lord and personal Savior (1 Peter 2:9).

I welcome you to pray this prayer if you have not accepted Jesus Christ as your Lord and personal Savior:

> *Dear Lord Jesus, I acknowledge that I am*
> *a sinner and I need a savior.*
>
> *I accept Jesus Christ as my Lord and Savior today.*
>
> *I believe that He died for my sins and on the*
> *third day rose again from*
>
> *the dead and is now seated at the right-hand*
> *side of God, interceding for me.*

Welcome to the family of God if you prayed the above prayer. You are now a Child of God (2 Corinthians 5:17). I pray and cover you in the blood of Jesus. I ask that God order your steps and direct your path all the days of your life, that you would be rooted and grounded in the Word of God and have fellowship with the Holy Spirit.

Find a Bible-believing church to fellowship with, be committed to and grow in your faith. Read your Bible and pray every day.

I welcome you to the Kingdom of God in Christ Jesus. You are now a citizen of heaven.

SCRIPTURE REFERENCES

Chapter 1: ¹Matthew 7:7-8
²Ephesians 4:8 ³Luke 18:1
⁴Luke 11:1 ⁵Luke 9:18; Acts
3:1 ⁶Ephesians 6:12

Chapter 2: ¹Psalms 100:3;
Matthew 5:45; Luke 15:12-15
² 1John 2:27 ³II Chronicles.
7:14 ⁴Daniel 6:10; Acts
2 ⁵ 2 Corinthians 10:4 ⁶
Matthew 11:12; Luke 11:5-8
⁷1Chronicles 4:9; Genesis
32:26 ⁸ James 5:17 ⁹ Luke
18:1-8 ¹⁰Revelation 12; 1
Peter 5:7 ¹¹Acts 12:5-17; 1
Kings 18:17

Chapter 3: ¹John 10:10 ²Josuah
24:15 ³Isaiah 55:11; Romans
10:17 ⁴Jeremiah 1:12 ⁵1 Peter
2:24; Psalms 118:17 ⁶Romans
8:37; 1 Peter 2:24; 2 Cr. 8:9;
Isaiah 54:17 ⁷ Isaiah 53:5;
Jeremiah 29:11 ⁸Romans
8:28 ⁹Matthew 26:39; Psalms
106:15 ¹⁰James 4:3 ¹¹1 Kings
17 ¹²Ecclesiates 3:11; 1
Corinthians 2:9 ¹³Hebrews 14:2

Chapter 4: ¹Matthew 6:6
²1 Timothy 2:1-3; Genesis
18:23-32; Exodus 33:12;
Daniel 9:3 ³Acts 12:5-6

Chapter 5: ¹1 Corinthians 2:9-14
²John 1:14; Colossians 1:15-17;
2:3 ³Ephesians 1:18,19 ⁴Genesis
21:15-20 ⁵Romans 8:17 ⁶II
Samuel 9; 16; 19:26⁷Hosea
4:6; II Samuel 9:7 ⁸I Samuel
23:2; II Samuel 2:1 ⁹Hebrews
4:16 ¹⁰Psalms 23, 37:23 ¹¹Acts
16:9, l0 ¹²2 Corinthians 10:3;
1 Timothy 4:2; Luke 22:31;
Ephesians 6:12 ¹³II Kings 6:12
¹⁴Nehemiah 6:12-13 ¹⁵Romans
8:31 ¹⁶Acts 4:29-31

Chapter 6: ¹1 Corinthians
14:15 ²Acts 2:7-11 ³John
11:41,42 ⁴Acts 2:4; 1
Corinthians 14:2 ⁵Acts 19:6
⁶Ephesians 6:18; Romans
8:26 ⁷1 Corinthians 14:26
⁸Luke 18:1; 1 Thessalonians
5:17 ⁹John 4:24 ¹⁰Ephesians
5:18,19 ¹¹1 Samuel 1:12,13

Chapter 7: [1]Luke 4:1-2 [2]Ezekiel 8:21,23; Esther 4:15,16 [3]Matthew 9:15, 17:21; II Corinthians 12:9 [4]Isaiah 58:1-12 [5]Hebrews 10:38; Romans 1:17; Habakkuk 2:4; 1 Corinthians 13:13 [6]Hebrews 11 [7]Romans 10:17 [8]Luke 1:38 [9]II Timothy 2:13; Jeremiah 1:12 [10]James 1:6-8 [11]Matthew 17:20; Luke 17:5 [12]Hebrews 11:32-40 [13]II Timothy 1:7 [14]Isaiah 41:10 [15]Acts 1:8, 4:1-13 [16]Luke 2:52; 1 Samuel 2:26 [17]Esther 5:7-8 [18]Psalms 105:17; Daniel 1:9 [19]1 Samuel 16:1;11

Chapter 8: [1]Romans 12:1 [2]John 14:3; Matthew 5:8; Romans 14:17; Hebrews 12:14 [3]Isaiah 59:2; Jeremiah 5:25; 1 John 1:5; II Corinthians 6:14 [4]Leveticus 11:44; Galatians 2:20 [5]1 Peter 1:15, 2:9 [6]Matthew 5:16 [7]Galatians 5:19-26 [8]Romans 6:4 [9]John 4:24 [10]Matthew 24:12; James 4:4; II Peter 2:7-8 [11]Hebrews 12:16-17 [12]James 5:16; Isaiah 38:2-7; Revelation 22:10-12 [Extra]Acts 26:18, Romans 13:12, Ephesian 5:8, Colossians 1:13, Revelation 21:8, 22:15

Chapter 9: [1]Jeremiah 33:3; Psalms 4:4, 66:18-20 [2]Psalms 46:10 [3]Exodus 14:13 [4]1 Kings 19:12, 13 [5]Psalm 62:11 [6]Matthew 6:8 [7]John 16:24 [8]Proverbs 14:12 [9]Matthew 7:11; James 1:17 [10]II Samuel 2:19; Psalms 106:15; Numbers 22:32-35 [11]Daniel 10:13 [12]Psalms 104:27; Isaiah 55:8, 9 [13]Habakkuk 2:3

Chapter 10: [1]Psalms 62:11 [2]Genesis 17:1; 16:13; 22:14; Exodus 15:26; Judges 6:24 [3]Numbers 23:19-20 [4]1 Kings 19:11-12 [5]Deuteronomy 29:29; 1 Corinthians 13:9 [6]Daniel 10:12-13 [7]Romans 9, 9:13(Amp) [8]Genesis 27; Proverbs 4:23; Luke 2:35; Hebrews 4:12 [9]Genesis 3 [10]Job 38 [11]Malachi 3:6

Chapter 11: [1]Judge 6:11-16 [2]Matthew 13:12; Luke 12:48; Philippians 3:13 [3]John15:5

ABOUT THE AUTHOR

Gabriel is an ordained minister of God with a mandate and passion for souls. His experiences in prayer have brought him answers that others call "coincidences." Because of this, he loves to pray, because more "coincidences" occur. He grew up loving God, and he has never shied away from the testimony of how God picked him from a zero to be an end-time firebrand minister. His Apostolic ministry allows him to bless the body of Christ. As a conference speaker, his passion for youth is to inspire them to attain excellence. Currently, he lives in the United States as the Bishop-Elect for Alive Chapel International.

Trained as Accountant and Administrator, he holds an MA in Theology from Central University (Ghana) and an MBA from Birmingham City University (UK). He is married to Darling Priscilla Jehu-Appiah Donkor, and they are blessed with three children: James, Jasmyn and Joella.

He can be contacted by email at: angel24us@yahoo.com, or gabrieldonkor187@gmail.com.

www.ingramcontent.com/pod-product-compliance
Lightning Source LLC
Chambersburg PA
CBHW032011040426
42448CB00006B/589